SHELLFISH COOKBOOK

SHELLFISH COOKBOOK

by Phillip Mason

DRAKE PUBLISHERS, INC.   New York

Published in 1974 by
Drake Publishers Inc.
381 Park Avenue South
New York, New York 10016

Library of Congress Cataloging in Publication Data

Mason, Phillip.
    Shellfish cookbook.

    1. Cookery (Shellfish) 2. Shellfish. I. Title.
TX753.M37   641.6'9'4   74-6080
ISBN 0-87749-677-3

Printed in the United States of America

1820862

Contents

Acknowledgments

I WOULD like to pass on my personal gratitude and thanks to the many people who have contributed to my small fund of knowledge on the subjects of shellfishing, shellfish, and the cookery of shellfish. Special thanks are due to Capt. Bill Eaton who taught me the art of "scalloping"; my brother Ed and his wife Ann; Bruce Bagley with whom I have enjoyed many superb shellfish dinners, and from whom I have learned much about shellfish; and also my good friend Jimmy Kerrigan, a shellfisherman from Cape Cod who has provided me with some of his good recipes and as much lore on the subject of shellfishing.

Introduction

LIVING CLOSE to the sea, as I do, affords me the pleasure of both the availability of a wide variety of fresh shellfish, and the pleasure of digging and catching my own. The pleasure that is derived from collecting your own fresh shellfish is at best a difficult one to describe. For me there is no other place in the world where I can find as much relaxation, peace of mind, or escape from the strifes of everyday life than at the seashore. The sea, with its many moods, and soft whispers of the as yet unsolved mysteries stirring in mens' souls, has an attraction for most people which is difficult, if not impossible, to describe in mere words.

If you do not live by the seashore, it is still possible to obtain most of the delicacies of the sea dealt with in this book, from your local fish market or supermarket. The modern day miracles of packaging and transportation allow you to obtain, from the aforementioned sources, a liberal selection of fresh, frozen, or canned shellfish during any season of the year. All you will lose by foraging for your shellfish from the supermarket shelf, is, the fun of going down to the seashore and gathering your own supply, free of cost. Indeed, this is a great deal of fun lost, from my point of view. As for the recipes that I have included in this book, you can use the fresh, frozen, or canned materials equally as well as the freshly caught ones.

In this book I shall also describe how you can find, identify, catch, open, and cook all of the popular shellfish that are to be found on almost any coastal sea beach or mud-flat in the United States. Included are many of my favorite recipes which are basically simple, fast, and easy to prepare. In presenting these recipes, I have in no way tried to be fancy or spicy. The recipes are, for the most part, old and traditional ways of preparing the particular shellfish described in each recipe, and none will be found to be beyond the skills of any normally competent cook. With these recipes, you should be able to turn out some memorable seafood feasts which will always be relished by your family and others who find themselves sitting at your table.

With the high prices of protein rich materials being what they are these days, I would like to stress an important fact regarding the virtues of fish as well as shellfish. Fish is not a substitute for meat—fish is meat. The shellfish products mentioned in this book are generally regarded as complete protein foods, as are all fish, whether of the fresh or saltwater variety. Incidentally, fishy things are quite rich in vitamin B, while many also contain a high proportion of vitamins A and D.

It is my fond hope that through this book I may help to bring a few persons to know the joys of foraging for their own shellfish, as well as the culinary joys that can be derived from a fondness for all types of shellfish. It is toward this end that I have provided the information contained in this little book.

SHELLFISH COOKBOOK

Chapter One

Clams

ABOUT CLAMS

CLAM IS the popular name of many widely varying edible bivalve mollusks. In the United States one commonly designates either the Quahog (Venus mercenaria), the hard or round clam, or else the Manninose (Mya arenaria), long or soft clam. The Quahog has a heavy, glogose shell, related to the cockles, and plows its way along sandy bottoms, standing erect on its thin edge. Quahogs are obtained almost wholly by raking, in water up to 40 feet in depth. They abound from Cape Cod to Florida, and in localities around the Province of New Brunswick, Canada. Great Britain has the "Gaper," a closely related species, but it is not as popular as a food item. The "giant clam" of the East Indies (Tridacna gigas) is the largest of living mollusca; its soft part often amounting to 20 pounds of edible flesh, while the deeply hollowed shells may weigh up to 500 pounds. Some Catholic churches use the shells of the giant clam to hold Holy water. This use well accords with the beautiful pearly white color of the inner surface of the shell.

Small clams and quahogs, often eaten on the half-shell, are, along with oysters, the only animals eaten alive by North Americans.

There are about 15,000 species of the clam family throughout the

1

world and all of them are edible, although many are not sufficiently abundant to have become popularized as foodstuffs.

ANATOMY OF A CLAM

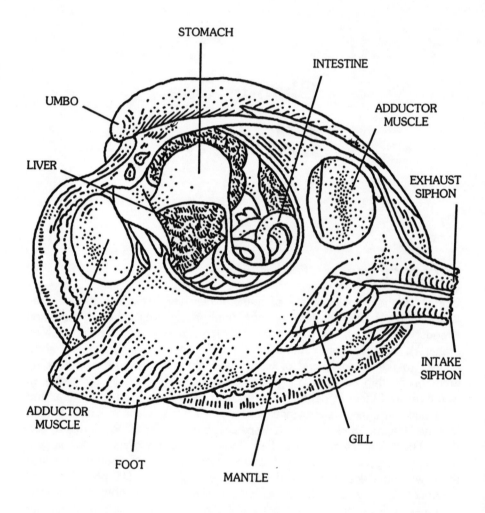

IDENTIFYING THE COMMON EDIBLE CLAMS

THE QUAHOGS

Quahogs

Quahogs are the hard-shelled round variety of clam which must be at least 3 inches in diameter or larger to be classified as a Quahog. Being the least tender of their kind, these large sized Quahogs are best used in chowders, stuffed clam recipes, etc.

Littlenecks

These are the same as Quahogs, the only difference being that they are younger and smaller. They must be about 1½ inches in diameter to fall into the Littleneck classification. They are the tenderest of the hard-shelled clams and are the most suitable for eating raw on the half shell.

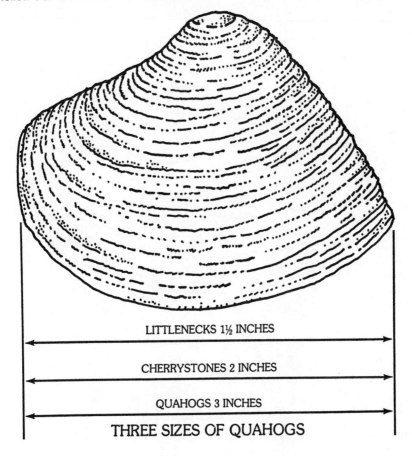

LITTLENECKS 1½ INCHES

CHERRYSTONES 2 INCHES

QUAHOGS 3 INCHES

THREE SIZES OF QUAHOGS

Cherrystones

Cherrystones are the third classification of the hard-shelled clams commonly called Quahogs. They are between Quahogs and Littlenecks in size, about 2 inches in diameter. Cherrystones are also quite tender and can be used in any of the recipes contained in this book with good results. Cherrystones make an especially excellent feed of steamed clams, and are the preferred size of Quahog for this purpose.

SOFT-SHELLED CLAM

The soft-shelled clams are elongated in shape and have a black colored neck. They are often referred to as steamers, longnecks, blacknecks, or just plain clams.

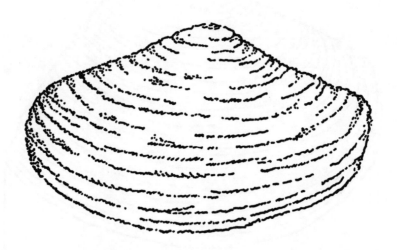

SOFT-SHELLED CLAM

SURF CLAM

Surf clams, which prefer the environment of a sandy, surf pounded shoreline, tend to be rather large in size with 7 inches long shells being quite normal. The surf clam is not a deep burrower; found only a few inches below the surface of the sand at the extreme low tide level, and even extending further, a depth of 10 feet underwater, at low tide. Their shell is rather coarse and very whitish in color, although they may have a light brown scum over their shells when still alive. Surf clams are gathered for food in many areas along both the Atlantic and Pacific coasts by those who know of their delicate culinary possibilities. After severe storms beaches are often strewn with thousands of surf clams washed up by heavy seas.

The meat of a surf clam is not to be used whole as a substitute for other clams. As with the scallop, it is only the adductor muscles that is used for eating. The surf clam has two adductor muscles as opposed to only one in a scallop. These tender little morsels are about 1 inch in diameter by 1 inch long, and after trying them I am sure you will agree that they are much superior to the scallop in all respects.

When gathering surf clams, keep only those which are 5 or more inches in diameter. The smaller ones do not contain enough meat to be worthwhile, and if thrown back you can help insure a future supply at your favorite clamming area.

When opening surf clams, follow the same procedure as with scallops—that is, keeping your knife blade close against the inside portion of the shell so that it slides underneath the adductor muscles and does not cut them in half. Once you have slid your knife under and over both adductor muscles, they can be easily removed with your fingers, as they are only very lightly attached to the rest of the clams' substance.

You can use the meat of surf clams in any way that you would scallops, or other shellfish dishes for that matter. Although the adductor muscles are the only part of the surf clam commonly eaten, a passable chowder or stuffed clam can be made by grinding up the entire contents of this clam into as find a consistency as possible. You will find that the tender little adductor muscles are quite delicious eaten raw—yes, even better than scallops or cherrystone clams. Be sure to save some of the natural juice from your surf clam while you are shucking them; you will find it one of the very best clam juices you have ever tasted.

There are many common names in use in various localities to identify the surf clam: Bar clam in most of Canada; hen clam in Maine; sea clam in parts of Massachusetts; also surf clam, beach clam, or skimmer clam in the mid-Atlantic states.

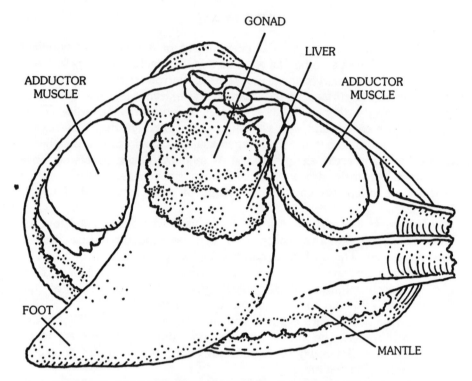

EDIBLE ADDUCTOR MUSCLES OF THE SURF CLAM

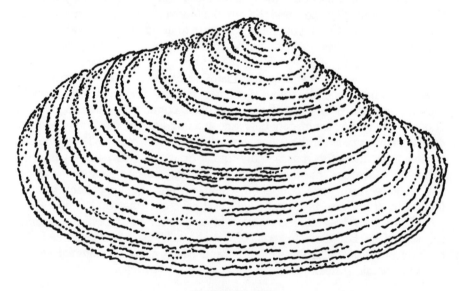

SURF CLAM

THE PISMO CLAM

The famous pismo clam, found only on the west coast of the United States, is highly prized for its savory flavor and tenderness. These clams are found only on the open, sandy beaches from mid-California southward to the southern portions of Mexico.

The pismo clam is so extraordinarily good that it can be used in any recipe calling for clams with absolutely mouth watering results.

Pismos are so adored by Californians that commercial diggers have reduced their numbers to the point where lawmakers have finally had to clamp down dramatically on the numbers that may now be taken. Even with these strict conservation laws, the pismo clam is still in very real danger of completely disappearing from California's beaches. As of this date, only 15 clams daily may be dug by any one person, and no clam smaller than five inches in diameter may be kept. However, this limit is quite reasonable as each pismo clam of five inches in diameter will weigh in the neighborhood of about two pounds (including shell), and 15 of these will make a grand meal for any average sized family.

Pismo clams take from 4 to 7 years to grow to a legal size, and can be readily identified by their almost triangular shaped, brown to grayish colored, shells.

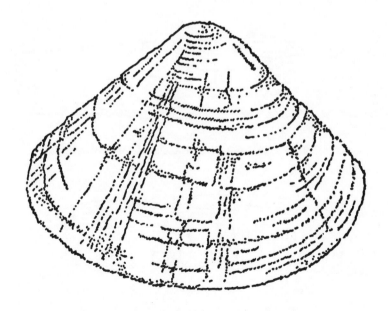

THE PISMO CLAM

RAZOR CLAMS

Razor clams obtain their name not only from their shape, which looks like an old fashioned straight razor, but also for their sharpness: their shells are indeed as sharp as razors and the Indians are reputed to have used them to shave with.

Razor clams are widespread on both the Atlantic and Pacific coasts of the United States and Canada. They are usually found in sand bars and sand banks very close to the low water mark. They live in a vertical position and often protrude out of the sand for about half their length when feeding. You may be able to spot them in this position just as the tide begins to come in, and if you proceed cautiously, you will be able to simply reach out and snatch them up. If you don't catch them when they are in this position, they may simply be dug in the same manner that you would dig soft-shell clams. They can usually be located by their rectangular shaped vent holes in the sand, which, will squirt juice when you step down firmly nearby, just as the soft-shelled clams are prone to do. When digging razor clams you will have to dig fast and deep; these critters are super fast burrowers and can really move. You will find them one of the most elusive clams that you will ever go after. If is a good idea, when digging razors, to wear a pair of gloves to prevent your hands from becoming a mass of tiny, and darn sore cuts.

STOUT TAGELUS VARIETY OF RAZOR CLAM—2-3½ INCHES

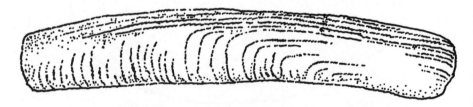

ATLANTIC RAZOR CLAM—UP TO 10 INCHES LONG

COMMON RAZOR CLAMS

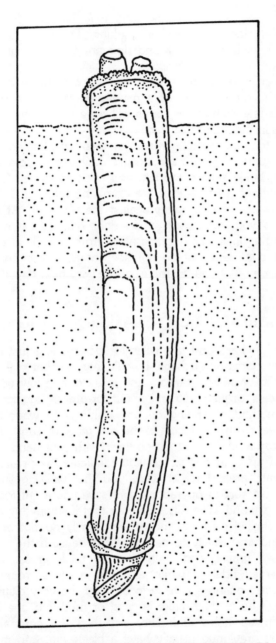

FEEDING POSITION OF THE RAZOR CLAM

MAY BE AS MUCH AS ONE HALF ITS BODY LENGTH OUT OF THE SAND ON INCOMING TIDES.

Razors are really good eating, and may be used in the very same ways that other clams are used in cooking. The foot and body portions can be eaten raw, but the neck and rims are a little tough to be gobbled up in this way.

Before opening a batch of razor clams, place them in a pail of fresh water to which you have added a handful of salt and a handful of corn meal. Within a few hours your clams will have purged themselves of sand and grit that is in their digestive tracts.

The best tool for opening razors is a round handled teaspoon, held with the bowl part in your hand, facing downward. Holding the clam in your left hand, hinge side to the left, and neck end away from you, insert the spoon handle just in back of the clam's neck. Slide the spoon handle towards you, while pressing lightly against the top shell. At the end of the shell nearest to you, turn your spoon right side up without removing it from between the shells, and scrape away from you. That's all there is to it. Razors are one clam that do not keep at all well in the shell, so use them the same day that you dig them, or the very next day at the latest.

DIGGING HARD-SHELLED CLAMS (QUAHOGS)

There are no hard and fast rules for determining just where you will locate a bed of clams or quahogs. I would suggest that you search around at likely spots in protected harbors and inlets during low tides. You might also ask the locals, or just keep an eye out for others digging.

A good method of finding quahog clams is to wade around during low tide and feel for hard objects in the soft mud, or sand, with your toes. If you run across a hard object, reach down with your hand and investigate; you might turn up a quahog which would indicate the presence of a "bed" in the immediate area. I might warn you that wearing sneakers (tennis shoes) during this sort of operation might save you a cut foot. Clam shells can be quite sharp and will easily slice your foot if stepped upon.

The hard-shelled clams of the quahog family do not bury themselves very deeply, and are usually to be found just beneath the surface of mud, soft sand, loose gravel, and even beneath thick grass. They generally thrive in protected tidal estuaries, and salt ponds surrounded by marsh grass. Often times quahogs can be located by the very distinctive, though nondescript vent holes they make in sand or mud. No one can teach you exactly what these holes look like, but they are generally tiny round holes, which, in grey mud usually have a black rim, and in black mud a grayish rim. However, don't count on finding these holes all the time— as often as not they will not make any hole at all.

When you locate a bed of quahogs, you can usually obtain excellent and very speedy results by employing a clam rake for gathering your quahogs. Simply drag this rake (see illustration) along the bottom, at about a 45 degree angle, and you will scoop up any quahogs that are there.

I would like to point out one thing here, as I will throughout the book, so that you don't miss or underestimate the importance of these warnings. Clams, as well as all other shellfish, must be alive right up to the moment of cooking, or eating raw on the half-shell. Always discard any dead ones, or ones in which the meat has a dried out appearance after prolonged storage in your refrigerator. Quahogs with broken shells are perfectly safe to eat if eaten the same day as they are dug.

Caution: Collect quahogs only from waters that you know for certain to be un-polluted. This warning is very important and holds true for all other types of shellfish as well.

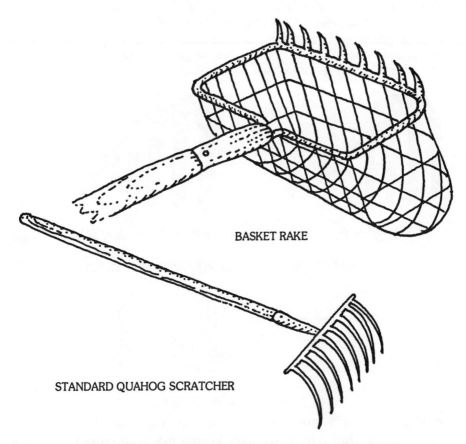

BASKET RAKE

STANDARD QUAHOG SCRATCHER

SOME TOOLS USED FOR DIGGING QUAHOGS

DIGGING SOFT-SHELLED CLAMS

The soft-shelled variety of clam is by far the tenderest and sweetest clam that the sea has to offer, however, it is far less comon these days than the hard-shelled clams of the quahog variety. If you should come across a bed of soft-shelled clams, you can adapt them to any recipe calling for clams equally as well as you can the more commonly found quahog or other types of clam.

The soft-shelled members of the clam clan dwell at the low tide line, and almost always reveal their presence by the tiny vent holes that they make in the sand. If you drop a heavy rock, or step down firmly in the vicinity of these holes, the clam will squirt a little stream of tobacco colored juice up through the hole to let you know whether or not he is at home Dig at that spot immediately and you should come up with one of the best eating clams of all for your efforts. You may have to dig deep for this fellow, as it will surprise you at what depths these burrowers can be found. Digging only a few inches down into the sand will usually prove disappointing. Like all good things, it takes work to get at these juicy and delicious little clams, but the reward is well worth the effort.

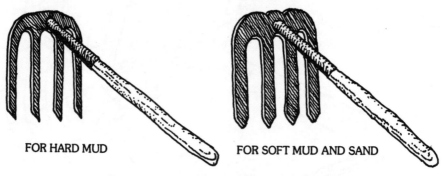

FOR HARD MUD   FOR SOFT MUD AND SAND

EXAMPLES OF SOFT-SHELLED CLAM DIGGING TOOLS

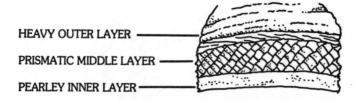

HEAVY OUTER LAYER ———

PRISMATIC MIDDLE LAYER ———

PEARLEY INNER LAYER ———

THE LAYERS OF A CLAM SHELL

A clam shell has 3 distinct layers, all of which are manufactured by the mantle of the clam. The tough outer layer is mainly to protect the middle layer from the small amounts of corrosive acid that are present in all sea water.

HOW A CLAM BURROWS INTO SAND AND MUD

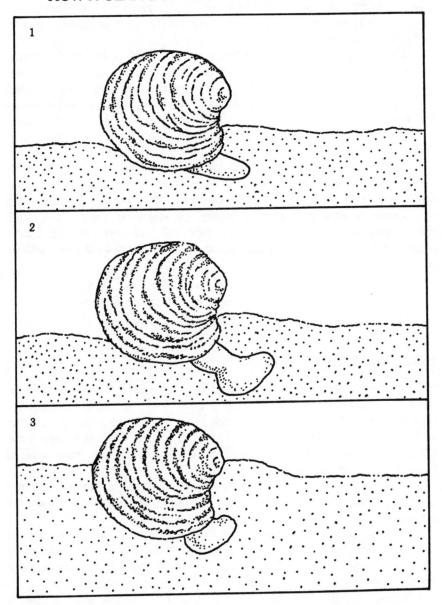

(1) Clam extends foot into sand. (2) Clam expands foot which acts as an anchor. (3) Clam then shortens foot, thus pulling itself into the sand. Clams such as the soft-shelled clam and the razor clam can perform this operation with amazing speed.

The soft-shelled clams make the very best steamed clams of all, and indeed it is for this reason that they are often referred to as "steamers." Served with melted butter as a dip, there are no finer steamed clams to be had in the world.

When digging soft-shelled calms, you may break a few of the shells. These broken clams are perfectly alright to eat if you are going to eat them the same day that you dig them. The one problem with broken shelled clams is that it's next to impossible to rid them of the sand and grit that has found its way inside them. I usually feed them to the seagulls which are invariably hanging around licking their chops at my bucket full of clams.

When you get your bucket of clams home, proceed with the corn meal soaking as you would for razor clams. They are then ready for opening, steaming, or storage. Almost all clams will keep quite well for a week or 10 days, if stored in your refrigerator's vegetable chiller. They will remain good as long as they retain their moisture and close up tightly when handled. Any clams which appear to have begun to dry out should be discarded.

Caution: Again I want to stress the importance of digging for clams only in waters that you know for certain are free from pollution.

HOW TO OPEN CLAMS

First place the clam in the palm of your left hand (if opening quahogs, place the short end nearest to your thumb). Insert a thin knife blade between the two shells and maneuver the blade so that the knife can cut the adductor muscles which are located near the hinge. The clam uses these adductor muscles to keep his shell closed, and once you have severed them, the shell will pop open.

If you are going to eat them raw right on the spot, remove the top shell and scoop under the meat with your knife blade, to loosen the connecting tissue, and simply slurp it down.

If you bounce a calm around, or treat it all roughly, you will come to appreciate where the term "clam up" came from. If a clam should resist all your efforts to open it, just stick him under hot running water for a minute or so and he will soon come around to your way of thinking.

Incidentally, the best way to determine if a clam is alive, is that it closes up tightly when handled and cannot be pulled apart by hand. Dead clams are usually gapping open, or can be easily opened with your fingers. This is because the adductor muscles no longer maintain their iron like grip after the clam has died.

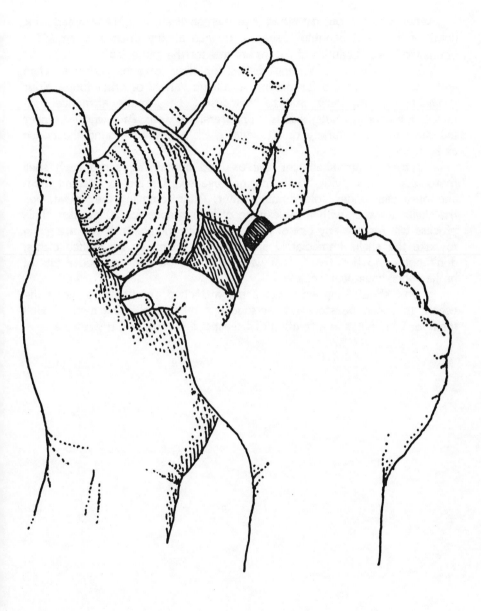

THE CORRECT METHOD OF OPENING A CLAM OR QUAHOG

USING CLAM SHELLS AS DISHES

When you are out gathering your own shellfish, you are also acquiring some of the most beautiful dishes to be had at any price. It is an added bonus that these beauties of nature are free for the gathering.

Besides acting as serving dishes for their original contents, clam shells can also be used for stuffing an infinite variety of other foods. Your imagination is the only limit to their uses. They make attractive containers for candies, nuts, salads, appetizers, etc., etc. And who lives near the sea without a variety of attractive shells scattered around the house as ashtrays?

To clean clam shells for use as food containers, scrub each shell thoroughly with a wire brush (do not use soap) prior to opening them and rinse well under cold running water. After removing their meat, boil the shells in water with a tablespoon of baking soda for 20 minutes. This process will remove any bits of meat clinging to the shells. If you are going to bake the shells immediately after opening them, as for stuffed clams, don't bother to boil them. Just wash well and be sure any loose bits of broken shell have been removed.

If you should happen upon some attractive empty shells along the beach, they can be sterilized for food use by the following method: Boil them for 20 minutes in a solution of 1 teaspoon Clorox to 1 quart water.

CLAM RECIPES

CLAM CHOWDER

To a Yankee or Canadian it's chowder, but to a Frenchman it's la chaudière, which means "the big stew pot": a grand mixture of clams or fish, corn or peas, seasoned with pieces of bacon or pork, onions, and, of course, a few pinches from the spice shelf. Sometimes milk is added, and sometimes tomatoes (dyed-in-the-wool yankees don't even mention the fact that clam chowder can be made with tomatoes). Any way you spell it, or make it, clam chowder is a wonderfully declicious and hearty meal.

New England Clam Chowder #1

½ quart clams, shucked	1 quart hot milk (or light cream)
2 to 3 slices salt pork	2 to 3 cloves
2 small onions, chopped	1 dash allspice (optional)
6 large potatoes, thinly sliced	1 dash cayenne pepper (optional)
1 dash Worcestershire sauce (optional)	

Wash clams thoroughly to remove all sand and grit. Then place them into a kettle with about ½ inch of water in the bottom; cover and boil until the shells open. Pour off the liquid and save it. When clams are cool enough to handle, remove the meat from the shells.

Fry slices of salt pork and small chopped onions in the bottom of a kettle, and when done, pour in one quart of boiling clam liquor. Add large potatoes and cook until nearly done. Add in the clams, the hot milk (or light cream), and the salt and pepper. If the mixture seems too thick, add a bit more boiling water.

Cloves, allspice, cayenne pepper, Worcestershire sauce, and other seasonings may also be added, according to taste. Serve piping hot with crackers floating on the top of each individual serving bowl. Serves 6 to 8.

New England Clam Chowder #2

By doing a little experimenting with ingredients and seasonings, you will arrive at your own "secret" chowder recipe. The following is my favorite which I have worked out by this process of experimentation. Perhaps you will like it.

2 slices bacon

1 medium onion, chopped

2 medium potatoes,
   peeled chopped

Dash of pepper

1 pint shucked clams

2 cups milk

2 tablespoons butter (or margarine)

Crushed crackers

Chop bacon coarsely, place into a kettle and fry until nearly crisp. Then place a finely chopped onion into the kettle and cook until the onion is soft. Add potatoes to onion mixture along with salt, pepper, and 1½ cups water. Cook this mixture for about 15 minutes.

Drain the juice from your pint of shelled clams and put it aside for the moment. Chop clams coarsely. Add milk, clams, clam juice, and butter to the mixture in your kettle and simmer (do not boil) for about 5 minutes. Sprinkle crushed crackers over the top just before serving. Serves 4.

In order to prepare the clam recipes which are included in this book, you must, of course, have clams. Someone must dig them, and it somehow is becoming to the cook who has prepared a shellfish feast to be able to boast with pride, "I dug these clams myself."

Manhattan Clam Chowder

This dish is not rated very highly by most Cape Codder's but is certainly enjoyed by many others who find the addition of tomatoes to clam chowder a pleasant and tasty variation.

4 slices bacon

4 medium finely chopped onions

4 carrots, diced

1 can (1 pound, 14 ounces)
   tomatoes

1 pint shucked clams, chopped

2 teaspoons salt

Pepper to taste

2 bay leaves

3 medium potatoes, finely diced

1 teaspoon thyme

Cut the bacon into small pieces and fry in the bottom of a kettle until almost crisp. Add onions to bacon and cook until soft. Next add carrots and continue to cook over a low heat for 5 minutes, stirring occasionally.

Drain the tomatoes and place liquid in a measuring cup. Place drained tomatoes into kettle with the other vegetables. Drain clams and add the juice to the tomato liquid. Add enough water to the clam and tomato juice to make 1½ quarts of liquid. Pour this juice into kettle and season with salt, pepper, bay leaves, and thyme. Bring to a boil, lower heat, cover, and simmer gently for 45 minutes. Next add potatoes, cover the kettle again and cook another 20 minutes.

Add the clams and cook slowly, with the kettle uncovered, for 15 minutes.

This recipe makes about three quarts of chowder, and it will taste even better when reheated and served on the second day. Serves 6 to 8.

The largest pearl ever found was in the shell of a giant clam at Palanan in the Philippines on May 7, 1934. This pearl, known as the Pearl of Lao-tze, weighted 14 pounds and measured 9½ inches in length by 5½ inches in diameter. It is now locked in a San Francisco bank vault and is reputed to be valued at over four million dollars.

Clam Dip

1 can (7 ounces) drained minced clams or, 7 ounces finely chopped fresh clams
½ cup cottage cheese
Dash of Tabasco sauce
1 teaspoon finely chopped onion
Worcestershire sauce to taste
Salt and pepper

Chop clams up as finely as possible then mix all of the ingredients together. Serve cold as a dip for crackers or chips. Makes 3 cups.

Raw clams are about as easily digested as raw eggs and are considered a highly nutritious food to serve to children or invalids with digestive problems. They are equally good served steamed, baked, or in soups and stews if they have not been overcooked.

Quahog Stew

1 quart milk
½ cup butter
3 tablespoons flour
1 teaspoon chopped parsley
Salt and pepper to taste
1 quart quahogs with their juice, shucked
2 eggs, well beaten

Heat milk. Add 2 tablespoons butter, the flour, parsley, salt, and pepper to the heated milk, stirring well. Cook this mixture until it thickens, stirring often. Heat quahogs (or clams) in their own juice for 3 minutes then stir into the milk mixture. Place well beaten eggs and remaining butter into a large serving bowl; pour the stew over the top and stir well. Serve immediately. Serves 4 to 6.

The clam eating champion, according to the Guinness Book of World Records, is Joe Gagnon who ate 437 clams in 10 minutes at Everett, Washington in January, 1971.

Stuffed Clams

12 whole quahogs in their shells	Salt and pepper
5 heaping tablespoons butter	2 tablespoons chopped parsley
1 chopped medium onion	¾ cup bread crumbs

Wash quahogs thoroughly and place in a kettle with about ½ inch of water in the bottom. Cover and boil until the shells are open (about 3 or 4 minutes). Allow clams to cool and remove meat. Chop the meat into small pieces, drain, and set aside for the moment. Split shells in half; wash thoroughly, and trim away all muscle or bits of shell adhering to the shells. Melt 2 tablespoons of butter in a frying pan and fry the chopped onion for about 5 or 6 minutes. Add parsley, bread crumbs, chopped clams, remaining butter, and seasonings to taste. Stir and cook until bread crumbs are browned. Add enough clam juice to moisten. Spoon mixture into the 24 shell halves and place on a baking sheet. Bake at 375° F. for 5 minutes and serve hot right from the oven. Six of these stuffed shells should be plenty for each individual serving. Serves 4.

The growing period of a clam can be compared to that of any other crop; it extends from about the first of May through the first of December. During the clam's yearly growth period it may increase its volume by as much as nine hundred percent.

Cape Cod Quahogs Rockefeller

This recipe was given to me by Jim Kerrigan, who is one of the finest shellfish cooks I have ever run across. Jim claims that this recipe is a great favorite with the commercial shellfishermen of his area.

12 quahogs on the half shell (Cherrystones)
12 strips bacon
Cocktail sauce

First cook the strips of bacon until almost crisp. Then place a strip of bacon on top of each quahog on the half shell, and top with a dab of cocktail sauce. Place on a cookie sheet and broil for about 4 or 5 minutes. Serve hot right from the broiler. Serves 2.

See the chapter on shellfish sauces in this book for several recipes from which you can prepare a cocktail sauce. I would recommend Cocktail Sauce Number One for this recipe.

"Morning After" Cocktail

No need to explain the meaning of the title of this recipe, I hope. If you should ever have one of those mornings-after-the-night-before situations, try this cocktail; it really does help.

½ cup clam juice	2 raw clams
½ cup tomato juice	1 slice lemon

Thoroughly blend the juices together with crushed ice. Place clams in the bottom of a 10 ounce glass, pour in blended juices and add the lemon slice, giving it a squeeze as you place it in the glass. Serves 1.

In the miscellaneous shellfish recipe section of this book, you will find a few more delicious beverages that can be concocted with clam juice.

Steamed Clams

First thoroughly wash fresh clams (use soft-shelled clams, littlenecks, or cherrystones for best results). Place clams in a large saucepan or kettle with just enough water in the bottom to steam them open (about ½ cup). Cover tightly and steam until all the clams have opened their shells (about 8 to 10 minutes). Pour some of the broth from the kettle into a cup, add a big chunk of butter and a dash of pepper. Remove the meat from the clams and dunk it into this melted butter dip with a fork and enjoy the feast. Plan on 12 to 24 steamed clams per person.

Never throw away, or reject as food, the dark green or black mass located near the hinge end of a clam. This material is not dirt or feces, as some believe, but the liver, which is rich in glycogen and is the source of the sweet flavor and taste of fried clams.

Fried Clams

Many clam lovers prefer fried clams over any other method of preparing clams for the trip to the tummy. Here's how to do it, if you don't mind the little extra work involved.

1 egg, separated	½ teaspoon salt
½ cup milk	½ cup flour, sifted
1 tablespoon melted butter	24 shucked clams

Beat egg yolk and add to it half of the milk and all of the melted butter. Mix salt with flour and sift. Then stir into first mixture until smooth. Add remaining milk and fold in the stiffly beaten egg white; stir well and your batter is ready.

Drain the shucked clams and dip each one into the batter. Fry in deep fat until they turn a golden brown. Remove from fat and drain on absorbent towels. You will enjoy eating these with tartar sauce, catsup, just plain. Serves 2.

The largest known specimens of bivalve shells are those of the giant clam found in the central portions of the Pacific Ocean. One specimen found on the Great Barrier Reef in 1917, and now on display at the Museum of Natural History in New York City, measures 43 inches in length by 29 inches in width and weighs 579½ pounds.

Clam Fritters

4 eggs	1 cup flour
2 cups clams with juice,	2 teaspoons baking powder
shucked and chopped	1 pinch salt

Beat the eggs until foamy in a large bowl. Mix clams and clam juice in with beaten eggs. Sift flour, baking powder, and a pinch of salt together, and mix with clams and eggs. Fry this mixture as you would pancakes on a hot, well greased griddle. If the batter is too thick, thin with clam juice or water. Serves 4 to 6.

Remember that you can't cook shellfish tender, they are as tender as they will ever get when they are raw—so don't cook them long or hard as all you will accomplish by such action is progressively tougher and tougher meat.

Clamburgers

1 cup chopped clams	½ teaspoon salt
1 egg, beaten	1 dash pepper
1 tablespoon lemon juice	½ cup dry bread crumbs
1 tablespoon chopped onion	6 buttered hamburger buns

Combine all the ingredients except, of course, the buns and form into six flat cakes. Fry until browned on one side, then turn carefully and brown the other side. This should take about 10 minutes of cooking. Place between buttered, heated buns and serve. Makes 6.

Clam Custard

½ cup cold clam juice
3 eggs
2 cups clam broth

Beat ½ cup of cold clam juice with the 3 eggs. Place in a small baking dish and set into a pan of hot water. Bake at 325° F. for 20 minutes or until custard has set. When this custard has been chilled, cut into small squares, place into soup bowls, and pour hot clam broth over them. Serve immediately.

To make clam broth for this recipe, simply heat some clam juice and add 1 tablespoon butter per cup of juice. Seasonings may be added to taste. Serves 2.

The days of the part-time commercial clam digger are fast becoming numbered. The natural clam beds of commercial quantity and quality are fast being reduced by pollution, poaching, land development, and general overcrowding along our seashores. The shellfish business is more and more tending towards salt water farming operations for the growth and harvest of commercial shellfish crops. Shellfish are now being planted, cultivated, and harvested just like any other crop.

Sweet Clams

The Japanese are great lovers of clams, as well as all types of shellfish. I include this oriental dish which I think you will enjoy.

¼ cup Sake (Japanese rice wine) 2 dozen clams, shucked
3 tablespoons sugar   3 tablespoons soy sauce

Combine the sake, sugar, and clams in a heavy frying pan. Bring to a boil, stirring gently, over high heat. Cook for 3 minutes. Add soy sauce and continue to cook for 1 minute. Remove the clams from the liquid and set aside.

Boil the liquid in the frying pan for about 10 minutes, until it becomes syrupy. Add the clams and stir them into the syrup.

Place clams and sauce into a bowl and cool. This dish is best served chilled. Serves 2.

You can substitute shrimp, lobster, mussels, etc. for the clams to create interesting variations of this dish.

Hot Clam Broth

1 quart soft-shelled clams   1 dash of paprika
Salt and pepper to taste   Hot water

Scrub clams thoroughly to remove sand and grit. Place in a large kettle, add 1 cup water, cover, and cook for 10 minutes. Pour the juice through a strainer (a cheese-cloth lined colander does nicely). Add enough hot water to this strained liquid to make 4 cups. Add seasonings to taste and serve piping hot.

The clams, of course, should also be eaten, and could be served on the side with a butter dip. Serves 4.

Wampum

Upon the arrival of the white man in America, they found that the Indians already had a monetary system. This system was based on shell wampum instead of coins as the white man was accustomed to dealing with. Wampum consisted of strings of cylindrical beads that were carefully carved from quahog shells (Venus mercenaria). The blueish-purple portions of the quahog shell produced the most valuable wampum—the more readily available white wampum was only worth ¼ to ½ as much. The New England colonies finally ceased to accept wampum as legal tender in 1662, although as late as 1693, wampum was still accepted as payment for fares on the ferry to Brooklyn, New York.

Jellied Clam Broth

1 tablespoon non-flavored
  gelatin
1 cup clam broth, hot

Cold water
Parsley for garnish
1 wedge lemon

Soften up 1 tablespoon of non-flavored gelatin in a little cold water. Add 1 cup hot clam broth to the gelatin and stir until gelatin has dissolved. Set in refrigerator to jell. Serve with a garnish of parsley and a wedge of lemon. Serves 1.

Clam Gravy

Here is an easy to make and very tasty gravy that goes well over mashed potatoes, etc. It's easy and fast to prepare:

¼ cup salt pork or bacon
1 cup raw clams, finely chopped

1 cup water
¼ cup flour (approximate)

Fry some finely diced bits of salt pork or bacon until browned. Add clams and water. Cook until clams are done (5 or 6 minutes), then add enough flour to obtain the desired thickness. Makes 1½ cups.

Clams and Spaghetti

½ cup clam juice
1 package (10 ounced) spaghetti
2 cups cooked clams, shucked
      Salt and pepper to taste

⅓ cup butter
½ cup grated Parmesan cheese
1 pinch garlic salt

Add clam juice to water in which spaghetti has been boiled. Place clams, butter and seasonings in a frying pan and heat until fairly hot. Add grated cheese and blend well until mixture is thick. Add spaghetti (drained) and mix until coated evenly with sauce. Serve hot. Serves 2 to 4.

Clam Cakes

¾ cup sour cream
1 egg
1 cup cooked clams, minced

1½ cups flour
¼ teaspoon salt
1 pinch pepper

Mix together sour cream and egg. Add clams. Combine this mixture with flour and seasonings. Cook on a hot, well-greased griddle until browned on both sides. Serve topped with any sauce of your choice. Serves 2.

Cream of Clam Soup

1 cup minced clams with their   2 cups light cream (or milk)
   juice   1½ tablespoons butter
                        Salt and pepper to taste

Mix together clams, juice and cream. Heat but do not boil this mixture. Add butter and seasonings to heated soup and serve.
Garnish with small crackers and a sprig of parsley floated on top. Serves 2.

Cape Cod Clam Soup (easy style)

1 can (12 ounces) chicken broth
1 can (12 ounces) clam broth
1 cup minced clams, cooked

Combine chicken broth with clam broth and the clam meat. Heat through and season to taste. Serves 2 to 4.

Scalloped Clam Casserole

½ cup butter, melted   ¼ cup clam juice
2 cups soft bread cubes   Dash Worcestershire sauce
3 cups clams, shucked   2 tablespoons grated Permesan
   and drained   or Cheddar cheese
½ cup milk   Salt and pepper to taste

Combine melted butter and seasonings with bread crumbs. Place one third of this mixture in the bottom of a well-greased casserole dish and cover with half of the clam meat. Repeat for second layer.
Mix Worcestershire with milk and clam juice, then pour over the top of casserole. Top with remaining bread crumbs and the grated cheese. Bake in a 350° F. oven for 25 to 30 minutes or until browned. Serves 6.

Clam Souffle

4 tablespoons butter, melted   ½ cup clam juice
4 tablespoons flour   3 eggs, separated
½ cup milk   2 cups shucked clams, diced
Salt and pepper to taste

Blend flour and melted butter in the top of a double boiler over boiling water. Slowly add milk and clam juice, stirring constantly until sauce is thick and smooth (3 to 4 min.). Remove from heat and add beaten egg yolks. Place back over heat (low) and stir continuously for 1 minute. Remove again from heat and add seasonings and clams.

Fold stiffly beaten egg whites into the clam mixture and pour into a 2-quart, greased casserole dish. Set in a pan of water and bake in a 350° F. oven for about 45 minutes or until souffle is firm and top is browned. Serves 4.

Vegetable-Clam Drink

¼ cup tomato juice   1 stalk of celery
1 slice onion   2 cups clam juice

Mix all ingredients together in a blender for about one minute and serve chilled. Serves 2.

Clamato Juice

1 cup clam juice
2 cups tomato juice

Mix the two juices and chill thoroughly. This makes a great pick-me-up drink on hot days.

Clam Fizz

3 tablespoons clam juice   Soda water
4 tablespoons milk   Pinch of salt and pepper

Combine the clam juice and milk in a tall glass, add soda water to fill glass, top with a pinch of salt and pepper, then stir gently and serve cold. Serves 1.

Note: Clam juice spoils very easily and should always be kept on ice.

Hot and Spicy Clam Drink

1 teaspoon powdered ginger   2 tablespoons cream
    or cinnamon   2 tablespoons clam juice
                    1 teaspoon butter

Combine all ingredients in a mug, fill with hot water and serve. An added touch can be put to this drink by seasoning with a dash of celery salt. Serves 1.

Chapter Two

Oysters

ABOUT OYSTERS

OYSTER IS the common name of the edible bivalve mollusks of the family Ostreide, and especially refers to any of the numerous species of the genus Ostrea. The shells are irregular and unequal; the left shell (valve) is generally spacious, being strongly convex on the outer surface and noticeably excavated in the inside; the right valve is generally plane or concave externally, being always less convex than the left valve. Closely adhering to their inner surfaces are the two thin folds (mantle) of the body well. It is these folds which secrete the shell building material—the process being accomplished from within by successive layers, as well as along the margins of the shell to promote length.

Oysters feed on microscopic organisms which are washed into their gaping shells by the action of their gills and palps (see anatomy of an oyster). They live in "beds" or "banks" in depths generally from 18 to 120 feet.

The most extensive oyster beds of the United States are found in Long Island Sound and the Chesapeake Bay. The oyster is found, however, from the Gulf of St. Lawrence to and along the shores of the Gulf of Mexico, and also at points along the west coast, notably in the Puget Sound area and the Juan de Fuca Straits.

The age of an oyster can be determined from the layers which make up its shell—one layer per each year of growth. Oysters which are only one day old are so tiny that 1 million of them would hardly take up the area of the average persons little finger. If by chance all of those 1 million oysters grew up to edible size, they would equal more than four thousand bushels.

ANATOMY OF AN OYSTER

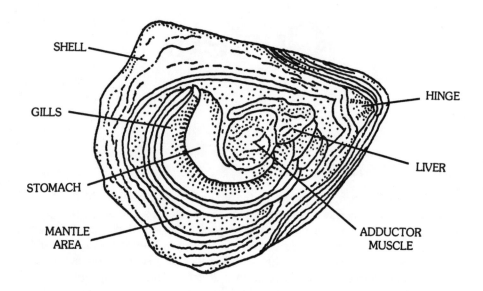

ANATOMY OF AN OYSTER—ENTIRE CONTENTS EDIBLE

BUYING OYSTERS

Oysters may be purchased for home use in their shells, or shucked (out of the shell). Ordinarily, they are obtainable in convenient half-pint, pint, or quart cartons. Oysters purchased fresh from the fish market should have a plump appearance, and should not show any signs of shrinking or shriveling up. Always examine oysters for pieces of shell which might be adhering to the meat, and always strain the liquid in which they come packed through a fine strainer. You may also purchase frozen oysters as well as canned or in the form of soups and stews.

GATHERING YOUR OWN OYSTERS

The saying that "oysters R in season," meaning that oysters should only be gathered during months that contain the letter 'R' in them (September—April), is probably due mainly to the fact that oysters spawn during these months. During the spawning season, when the water temperature is at its warmest, oysters tend to be thin and either tasteless or bitter.

The only equipment you will need for gathering oysters is a pair of gloves and a basket of some sort; though you may need a rake, or scoop if the water is more than knee deep.

Oysters are generally in short supply these days, but are not all that difficult to find if you have a bit of local knowledge about your particular area. Oysters most often grow attached to shell beds, rocks, pilings, and even other oysters. They are not burrowers and are never found under the surface of mud or sand. They do not move about.

Look for oysters in protected areas just underwater at low tide. You may occasionally find oysters exposed at those periods when the tides are exceptionally low. Oysters do not favor water that is too brackish (high in salt content) and are often found close to areas where fresh water streams empty into the sea.

Simply pull your oysters from the surface to which they are attached, and obtain your quota of legal sized oysters for a shellfish feast of the very choicest kind.

THE ENEMIES OF THE OYSTER

The very worst enemy of the oyster is not man, but a terribly innocent looking little snail with the sinister name of "oyster drill." It wreaks great havoc in oyster beds all during the year by boring holes through oyster shells whereupon it proceeds to feed on oyster flesh.

Indeed, oysters are surrounded by few friends and many powerful enemies. From the moment the spawn and milt are shed into the water, until the mature animal is placed upon your dining table, there is a constant gauntlet to be run. Many of the ova are not fertilized; of those that are, fishes and other animals swallow many, the mud of the bottom swallows more; after the young set (attach themselves to some object), star fishes, drills and whelks attack them; and when mature, beds of mussels are apt to cover them up and cut off their food supply, or man lays them away in great numbers with a touch of lemon or sauce to qualify their flavor. If not for the incredible numbers sent into the world every season, in a very short time there would soon be not a single oyster left in this world.

THE COMMON EDIBLE OYSTER

OYSTER DRILL—THE WORST ENEMY OF THE OYSTER

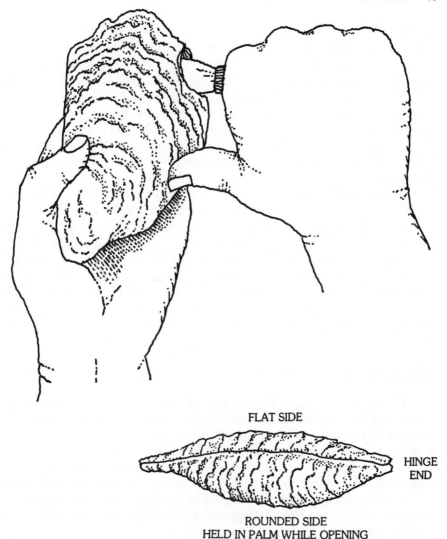

FLAT SIDE

HINGE
END

ROUNDED SIDE
HELD IN PALM WHILE OPENING

OPENING OF AN OYSTER AND SIDE VIEW OF OYSTER TO
SHOW ROUNDED AND FLAT PORTIONS OF THE SHELL

OPENING OYSTERS

Basically there are two different methods of opening (shucking)
oysters. The first is the chipping method: first knock off a bit of the lip

of the shell (see illustration) with a light blow of a hammer, then insert a knife between the shells and force them apart. The second method is to simply hold the oyster in your left hand, placing the more rounded half of the shell in your palm. About half way down the shell try to find the point the shell halves are joined. Wiggle your knife into this slit and locate the large adductor muscle, located near the widest edge of the shell. When you have cut this muscle, twist your knife and the shells will come apart.

In opening all shellfish, you should try to keep your knife blade tip as close to the upper portion of the inner surface of the shell as possible. This will keep you from lacerating the meat.

Knives used for opening oysters must be thin and made of good steel in order to do the job properly. Oysters are tough critters to open!

If you would like to open oysters in a manner that takes all the work out of it, here's a tip. Immerse oysters in carbonated water for about 5 minutes prior to opening. The carbon dioxide in the carbonated water gets the oysters quite drunk whereupon they completely relax the adductor muscles which hold their shells so tightly closed. When oysters are in this whacked out condition it is a simple matter to open them; you can shuck oysters with a speed that would astonish a professional shucker if he was unaware of your little secret.

COOKING OYSTERS

The meat, or flesh, of an oyster is composed almost entirely of a tender and delicate substance called albumen, and is free of tough muscles. In order to retain the tender qualities of the oyster, cooking must never be prolonged or done over a high heat. This sort of treatment will render the flesh into bubble gum consistency. Oysters should be cooked gently and quickly to retain their quality, delicacy, and ease of digestion. When preparing oyster dishes which require creams, sauces, or gravies, prepare and complete them first—then the oysters should be added and cooked only long enough to slightly curl their edges.

When serving oysters raw on the half-shell, use the deep half of the shells for serving dishes. Remember to save as much of their natural juice as possible to serve with them. The oysters' natural juice rivals the best clam juice in quality, but for some reason, it does not enjoy the same popularity.

There are many ways to prepare oysters after opening them, but some believe that the only thing that remains to do after opening them is to eat them. I suggest that you turn to the oyster recipe section and see what else you can do with the oyster besides slurping it down raw.

OYSTER RECIPES

Oysters are undoubtedly the "Mollusca Regal," and for this reason I have endowed this little book with more tidbits and recipes about oysters than any other single item. I am sure you will agree that the oyster deserves the lion's share of attention which it has earned from the gastronomic delights it has passed on to the dinner tables of mankind since before recorded history.

Fried Oysters   1820862

24 oysters, shucked
3 egg yolks
Dry cracker crumbs, crumbled

Remove oyster meat from shells and dry on soft absorbent towels (when dried they will not absorb grease). Gently beat the yolks of 3 eggs. Have enough hot grease ready in a deep frying pan to cover the oysters. Dip oysters in the egg yolk, then roll in finely crumbled cracker crumbs. Place a few oysters at a time into hot grease and brown. (Too many will cool the grease down too much.) Serve as hot as possible. Serves 2 to 4.

The common expression that "oysters are digestible" is derived from the fact that the protein of the oyster is composed of a very special carbohydrate derivative, consisting of glucogen. In addition to their high protein content, oysters are a little storehouse of minerals—containing such things as sodium, iodine, calcium, copper salts, and many others of importance to the human body.

Oyster Gumbo

2 tablespoons butter	½ teaspoon pepper
2 tablespoons flour	1 pinch thyme
1 small onion, chopped	½ teaspoon Worcestershire
2 tablespoons diced celery	sauce
2 tablespoons parsley, chopped	2 bay leaves
1 tablespoon salt	18 oysters, shucked

Melt butter in a small frying pan. Blend in the 2 tablespoons of flour, then add ¼ cup water and mix thoroughly. Cook for 10 minutes over low heat, stirring frequently to keep from scorching. Place liquid from oysters into a large saucepan. Add 6 cups water and all other ingredients, except oysters. Bring to a boil, then slowly add the flour mixture from frying pan, stirring it in well. Bring to a boil again and simmer for 30 minutes. Just before serving, add the oysters and heat for 5 minutes, or just until the oysters begin to curl at the edges. Remove from stove and serve immediately. Serves 4.

Scalloped Oysters

1 pound oyster meat, 1½ cups fine bread crumbs
   shucked and drained ¼ pound butter
Salt and pepper to taste

Cover the bottom of a well greased baking pan with a layer of oysters and dab thickly with bits of butter. Cover with a thin layer of bread crumbs, and sprinkle with salt and pepper. Keep the layers of bread crumbs as thin as possible. Repeat these layers, until the pan is full, or you have used up your oysters. Finish off with a top layer of butter and bread crumbs. Bake at 350° F. until nicely browned, and serve hot. Serves 2.

The first known person to form artificial oyster beds with Sergius Orata, way back in the halcyon days of the Roman Empire. He established his oyster beds at Baiae, during the period of Crassus the Orator, just prior to the Marsic war. Sergius was engaged in this sea farming of oysters, not for the gratification of his own palate, but for financial gain, and he was indeed quite successful in earning a large fortune by this exercise of his sea farming ingenuity.

Sauted Oysters

Place well drained oysters into a frying pan with a little melted butter. Cook the oysters just until their edges begin to slightly curl. Salt and season to taste after removing from frying pan.

Roasted Oysters

½ dozen large oysters
Salt and pepper to taste
1 teaspoon Worcestershire sauce

Wash oyster shells thoroughly. Preheat oven to 400° F. Place oysters in a baking pan and heat in oven until shells open (about 7 to 8 minutes). (If you're heating oysters on the half shell, it will also take about 7 to 8 minutes for them to roast.) Remove the top shell of each oyster (the flatter half) using gloves to keep from burning hands. Season each oyster with a dash of Worcestershire sauce, salt, and pepper. Serve hot. Serves 1.

Oysters en Brochette

2 cups fresh oysters, shucked	2 teaspoons lemon juice
5 tablespoons chili sauce	1 dash Worcestershire sauce
1½ teaspoons horseradish	1 dash salt and pepper

½ pound fresh whole mushrooms (or canned)

Drain juice from oysters. Combine chili sauce, horseradish, lemon juice, Worcestershire sauce, salt and pepper. Dip oysters in this sauce mixture and place mushrooms and oysters alternately on skewer sticks. Cover with remaining sauce and broil for about 3 to 5 minutes on each side, or until mushrooms become tender. Serves 6.

Some historians have claimed, with a great deal of exaggeration it would seem, that Emperor Vitellius was accustomed to eating more than five thousand oysters per day. The claim has also been made that Seneca "the Wise" consumed about three thousand per week—this would be within the realm of a more believable figure.

Such grand claims do, however, serve to point out the very real value that mankind has placed upon the oyster for many centuries. Even before the dawn of recorded history, oysters were devoured for food by man, as is evidenced by the huge mounds of oyster shells left behind in the garbage dumps of prehistoric man.

Simple Oyster Stew

2 quarts shucked oysters, with juice	1 quart milk
	Salt and pepper to taste

8 tablespoons butter

Strain the juice from the oysters, check the meat for bits of shell, and place oysters and juice in a large saucepan. Simmer over low heat for about 5 minutes. Add milk and heat, but do not allow to boil. Remove when heated, season to taste, and serve in bowls topped with a tablespoon of butter. Serves 8.

Thyme, cayenne pepper, or mustard powder may also be added as seasonings if desired.

Those who disguise the taste of an oyster with sauces of one kind or another, are not aware that oysters from different beds, even beds located close to each other in the same body of water, have distinctly different tastes.

Angels on Horseback

12 large oysters, shucked
6 slices uncooked bacon
Salt and pepper to taste

Drain the juice from oysters and cut bacon slices into halves. Place each oyster onto the top of a slice of bacon, sprinkle with salt and pepper, then roll the bacon around the oyster and pin it together with a toothpick. Place in a shallow baking pan and bake in a hot (400° F.) oven until bacon is crisp (8 to 10 minutes). Serves 2 to 3.

According to the Guinness Book of World Records, the world's champion oyster eater is Peter Jaconelli who consumed 500 oysters in the time of 48 minutes 7 seconds on April 27, 1972.

Pickled Oysters

Pickled oysters will keep for quite a long time in a well sealed jar, if stored in a cool place. They make an excellent appetizer, which, if you are not careful, will end up being a meal.

½ gallon shucked oysters
½ teaspoon peppercorns,
   coarsely ground

½ teaspoon mace, ground
1 dash white pepper
⅔ strong vinegar

Steam the oysters in their own juice until they just begin to curl at the edges. Drain. Add coarsely ground peppercorns, ground mace, white pepper, and vinegar to the juice. Allow this mixture to boil over high heat for 5 minutes. Then pour the hot liquid over the oysters in a clean glass jar. Leave uncovered until almost cold, then add a few slices of lemon and seal up the jar. Makes ½ gallon pickled oysters.

The oyster has been living on this good earth of ours for a long time. The fact that nature protects the helpless is certainly evidenced by the fact that the oyster still remains on earth alive and well, while nature has seen fit to relegate the mastodon and dinosaur to natural history museums as mere curiosity pieces.

Baked Oyster Soup

1½ quarts light cream	1 dozen crushed crackers
2 tablespoons butter	Salt and pepper to taste
1 stalk celery, diced	3 dozen oysters, shucked

Bring the cream just to the boiling point, then add butter, celery, and cracker crumbs. Season this mixture with salt and pepper to taste. Drop in the oysters, a few at a time, and when mixture is just about ready to boil again, pour it into a baking dish and place in the oven. Let it brown at 400° F., give it a quick stir then allow to brown again. Serve as hot as possible straight from the oven. Serves 6.

Cape Cod Oyster Chowder

1 quart oysters, shucked	2 tablespoons butter
6 potatoes, peeled and thinly sliced	1 tablespoon flour
1 onion, thinly sliced	1 teaspoon salt
1 cup water	1 dash pepper
	3 cups milk (or light cream)
crackers	

Strain the juice from the oysters through a fine sieve. Make certain that no particles of broken shell are mixed in with the meat. Boil the potatoes and onion in the oyster juice and water until tender. Melt butter and blend into the flour, salt, and pepper. Then add milk and stir well, but slowly, into the vegetable mixture. Add oysters and simmer the entire mixture for 3 minutes. Place small crackers into the bottom of serving bowls and pour the chowder over them. Serve hot. Serves 6.

There should be no waste in the contents of a freshly opened oyster. Every scrap of meat and juice is edible. Oysters have it all together—they are high in mineral content and food value, and are extremely easy to digest.

Oyster Stuffing
For Holiday Turkey

2 dozen oysters, shucked	1 stalk celery, chopped
2 tablespoons butter	½ tablespoon salt
4 cups bread crumbs	¼ teaspoon pepper

2 tablespoons parsley, chopped

Drain juice from oysters and rinse them well under cold water. Place butter and oysters into a saucepan and bring to the boiling point. Add bread crumbs, celery, seasonings and parsley and mix together carefully so as not to break up the oyster meat. This exotic and tasty stuffing is now ready to go into your bird. Makes 4½ cups (double the quantities of this recipe if you are planning to stuff a very large bird).

The ground work for the first U.S. experiments in oyster farming was laid by the state of Rhode Island. In June of 1779 this state set aside a portion of the public domain for the cultivation and propagation of oysters.

Creamed Oysters

1 tablespoon butter	1 pinch oregano
1 tablespoon flour	1 dash pepper
½ teaspoon salt	1 cup light cream

2 dozen oysters, shucked

To make the cream sauce for this recipe, melt the butter in a saucepan and into it mix the flour, salt, oregano, and pepper. Add the cream and cook, stirring constantly until smooth and creamy.

Drain juice from oysters. Place oysters in a shallow pan with a little juice and cook for 5 minutes, or just until their edges begin to curl. Add to heated cream sauce and serve. Serves 4.

Hang Town Fry

The hang town fry originated during the gold rush days in Placerville, California. This dish is now a specialty of water-front restaurants in the San Francisco Bay area.

2 dozen oysters, shucked
¾ cup flour
7 eggs

Cracker crumbs, finely ground
3 tablespoons butter
¼ teaspoon salt

1 dash pepper

Drain oysters and dry on absorbent towels. Dip each oyster into flour seasoned with salt and pepper. Beat 2 eggs and dip each oyster into egg then roll in finely ground crack crumbs. Bring the remaining butter to the sizzling point in a large frying pan. Place oysters into frying pan and brown on one side. Beat the remaining eggs and season with salt and pepper then pour them over the oysters in the frying pan. Allow to cook for about 1 minute then turn and brown other side. Serve hot. This makes a delicious breakfast dish for 2 and goes well with fried potatoes and bacon, or sausage.

It is reputed that back in the California gold rush days, a miner appeared one day at a bar and ordered a plate of raw oysters and a whiskey cocktail. This hearty fellow is attributed with being the inventor of the oyster cocktail. After downing his whiskey, the miner placed the raw oysters in his glass, topped them with some catsup, pepper sauce and salt and pepper then gulped them down with a lip smacking flourish. The bartender, seeing the possibilities, began to sell the oyster cocktails as a specialty of the house, and they have since been refined into the form of the favorite American dish that is so much enjoyed today.

Crouton Scalloped Oysters

2 cups oysters, shucked
¼ pound butter
¼ teaspoon ground ginger
¼ teaspoon pepper

¼ teaspoon garlic salt
4 cups bread cubes (¼-inch)
½ cup heavy cream
paprika

Drain oysters. Mix the oyster liquid with the butter, garlic salt, pepper, and ginger and heat thoroughly. Add bread crumbs a little at a time until mixed in well; add more oyster liquid or melted butter if necessary. Place mixture in a greased baking dish in five layers—starting and finishing the layers with bread mixture, and using the oysters as a filling. Pour cream over the top and sprinkle with paprika. Bake at 400° F. for 25 minutes, or until well browned. Serves 4 to 6.

Curried Oysters

3 dozen large oysters, shucked   1 small onion, finely chopped
1 cup oyster juice   1 stalk finely chopped celery
1 tablespoon butter   ½ teaspoon curry powder
                            1 pinch of salt

Drain oysters and reserve the liquid. You will need a cup of this liquid and can add water to what you have to make up the amount, if needed.

Melt the butter in a frying pan and saute the curry powder, onion, and celery in it. Add the 1 cup of oyster juice and simmer for 15 minutes; then add oysters and heat through. Serve hot with sauce coating each serving. This recipe will serve 2 hungry shellfish freaks.

Lord Baltimore Soup

2 cups oysters, shucked   2 tablespoons flour
2 cups chicken bouillon   1 dash Worcestershire sauce
2 tablespoons butter   Salt and pepper to taste
                    ½ cup light cream

Boil oysters in their own juice just long enough to barely cook them (4 or 5 minutes). Add 2 cups of strong chicken bouillon.

Melt butter in a saucepan and stir in flour; cook for a few minutes. Blend flour and butter into oyster mixture along with all the seasonings and cook for 5 minutes. Just prior to serving, add the cream and heat to the boiling point, but do not boil. Serve hot. Serves 3 to 4.

Oysters Bienville

¼ cup onion, minced   ¼ cup white wine
2 tablespoons butter   24 oysters on the half shell

2 tablespoons flour
½ cup chicken bouillon
¼ cup mushrooms
   (canned or fresh)
1 egg yolk, beaten

½ cup bread crumbs
1 tablespoon grated
   Parmesan cheese
1 teaspoon salt
1 dash pepper

Cook onion in butter with flour, stirring until mixture browns. Add chicken bouillon and mushrooms. Add beaten egg yolk and wine slowly to sauce. Stir rapidly for several minutes until it thickens.

Leave oysters in their shell halves. Drain off any accumulated juice. Place on a shallow baking tray in a 400° F. oven for 5 minutes. Remove from oven and pour some sauce over each oyster. Cover the top of each with bread crumbs and a sprinkle of grated cheese. Return to oven and heat through (about 5 min.). Serves 4.

Oyster Loaf

2 cups raw chopped oysters,
   drained
1½ cups soft bread crumbs
3 tablespoons onion,
   grated

3 tablespoons celery,
   finely chopped
½ cup oyster juice
2 eggs, beaten
½ cup light cream

Salt and pepper to taste

Combine all ingredients, mix well and press into a deep, well-greased loaf pan.

Bake in a 350° F. oven for about 45 minutes, or until loaf is firm and top is browned. Serves 6.

Oyster Bisque

1 pint raw oysters,
   shucked and chopped
2 tablespoons onion, chopped
2 stalks celery, chopped

¼ cup butter
¼ cup flour
3½ cups milk
Salt and pepper to taste

Heat oysters in their own juice along with onion and celery for 6 minutes. Melt butter in a saucepan and stir in flour until smooth and thick. Add milk slowly and cook over very low heat, stirring constantly until mixture is thick and smooth. Add oyster mixture, season to taste and serve piping hot. Bisque may be thinned with more milk if necessary. Serves 4.

Long Island Pan-Fried Oysters

1 pint raw oysters, drained   1 tablespoon lemon juice
4 tablespoons butter   Salt and pepper
                      Buttered toast

Place oysters in frying pan with ¼ cup of oyster juice and cook until edges begin to curl. Add butter, lemon juice and salt and pepper to taste. Bring to a boil. Serve on buttered toast. Serves 2 to 4.

Oyster Stuffed Mushrooms

8 to 10 large mushrooms   1 cup cooked oysters, chopped
2½ tablespoons butter   ½ teaspoon Worcestershire
1 tablespoon finely   sauce
   chopped onion   1½ cups soft bread crumbs
                      ¼ teaspoon salt

Chop mushroom stems into fine pieces and saute with onion in 2 tablespoons butter until tender. Add oysters, Worcestershire sauce, salt and bread crumbs. Stuff mushroom caps with mixture and place in a shallow baking dish with 1 tablespoon water in the bottom. Dab with remaining butter and bake in a 400° F. oven for 20 minutes. Serves 2.

Oyster and Cheese Dunky Dip

1 package (8 ounces)   ¼ teaspoon salt
   cream cheese   ¼ cup oyster juice
1 tablespoon Worcestershire   2 teaspoons lemon juice
   sauce   ¾ cup cooked oysters,
                                                      drained and minced

Blend together cream cheese, Worcestershire sauce, oyster juice and lemon juice. Add oysters and mix thoroughly. May be thinned with additional oyster juice if desirable. Makes 1½ cups.

Chapter Three

Scallops

ABOUT SCALLOPS

THE SCALLOP is a well-known bivalve, which utilizes only a single adductor muscle for opening and closing its shell. The valves (shell halves) are fan-shaped, the left often more or less flat, the right more markedly arched; both are marked with sinuous radiating ridges, to which the Latin name pecten refers.

Scallops have from 15 to 40 little blue or blue-green eyes located around the margin, just inside the shell edges, among numerous tentacles which often protrude beyond the shell's edge. Scallops are capable of swimming by clapping their shells together, scooping in water and quickly forcing it out the rear on either side of their hinge. By this action they swim forwards instead of backwards as one might at first suppose. The thick, disc-like adductor muscle is usually the only part of the scallop that is eaten in this country. However, in Europe the entire scallop is eaten.

The life span of a scallop is relatively short, seldom exceeding more than three years. However occasional specimens do live up to ten years of age.

There are two major varieties of the scallop; the large sea scallop and the much smaller bay scallop. Sea scallops may be as large as 8 inches in diameter, while bay scallops seldom attain more than a maximum diam-

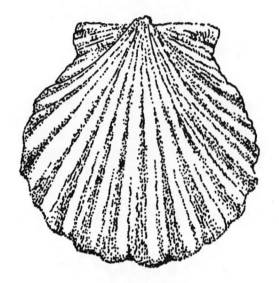

BAY SCALLOP

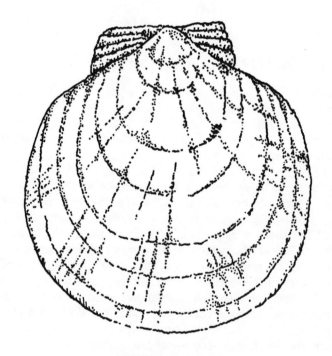

SEA SCALLOP

eter of 4 inches. However, both contain high levels of well balanced protein, little fat, and many minerals and vitamins necessary to our good health. The bay scallop is generally the tenderest of scallops and is the variety that concerns us in this book.

The color of the scallop shell varies widely, but is most often of a brown or blackish slate, orange, yellow-brown, reddish or purplish color. The lower valve (flatter half) is frequently a lighter color than the upper portion, or more convex shell half.

GATHERING SCALLOPS

By the time scalloping season rolls around (about October 1st) the sea is a bit too cold for wading in, so your first requisite for scalloping will be a boat. A small row boat will do nicely. In addition, you will need a long handled dip net with a fairly small diameter net and rather longish net bag. That's about all the equipment you'll need unless you want to invest in a glass bottomed box for viewing the bottom, or perhaps a pair of polarized sun glasses.

Scallops are not burrowers and will always be found lying on the surface of mud or sand, in shallow water. Grassy underwater areas are usu-

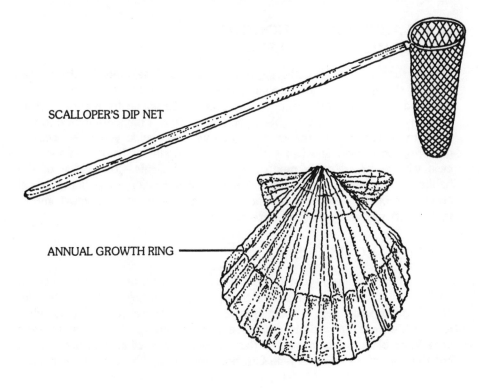

SCALLOPER'S DIP NET

ANNUAL GROWTH RING

ally the best locations, and you might have trouble seeing the scallops at first, as some older ones might have grass growing on their shells which disguises them somewhat.

When you locate a scallop, simply lower your dip net very gently and approach the scallop from the front. If the scallop panics at your approach, he will swim right into your dip net and will not readily be able to swim back out. Some scallopers like to approach them from the rear, and by giving them a little flip with the ring part of the dip net they fall right into the net with no trouble at all. You will soon learn a technique that appeals to you, and don't be surprised if you miss the first half dozen or so that you attempt to net.

It is best to get upwind of the area you plan to scallop over and allow the wind to slowly drift you over the area in water shallow enough for your dip net to operate in. Do not make any unnecessary disturbances which will panic the scallops and make netting them all the more difficult. In a good location you should be able to get a bushel of scallops by dip netting in about an hour, or an hour and a half. This amount will shuck out to somewhere around a quart and a half to two quarts of meat.

Only adult scallops are legal to catch (two years old) and they can be recognized by the distinct growth ring or hump like area on their shells.

SOME ADDITIONAL THOUGHTS
ON GATHERING SHELLFISH

Instructions for the gathering of shellfish are closely akin to the revelations of the secrets of good cooking. Each individual has his favorite methods, and despite the most expert advice one may obtain from books, experience is the surest and straightest path to success. I have attempted in this book to present the fundamentals which will help guide you to success in gathering your own shellfish with the least amount of trouble. Your success will be based on a mixture of four ingredients—knowledge of the habits of the species you are stalking; familiarization with the physical conditions of the seashore; proper collecting equipment; and, most importantly perhaps, a large dose of perseverance.

OPENING SCALLOPS

Hold the scallop in your left hand. Do be careful, as scallops are sharp shelled critters which can easily cut the hands. Insert a flexible bladed, round-ended knife just forward of the scallops hinge; twist slightly while forcing the knife upwards to cut the adductor muscle. Remember to keep your knife blade tight up against the inside of the shell so that you do not cut the adductor muscle in half. Cut both the top and bottom of the muscle where it joins the shell and your scallop will be opened. Pick out the round white muscle from the rest of the scallops innards and proceed with your next one. The round white muscle, which is the eating part, may vary in color from pure white to slightly pink, or occasionally yellow. No one seems to know why this color difference occurs, but it does not affect the taste or palatability in the least.

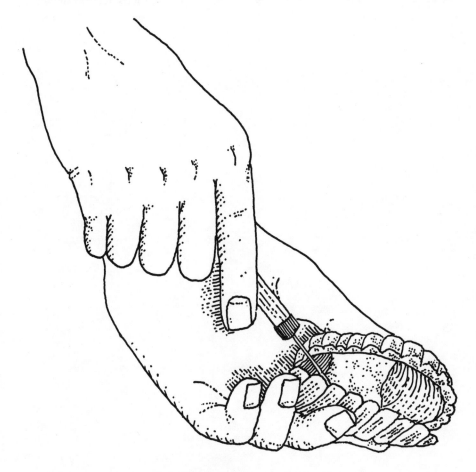

HOW TO OPEN A SCALLOP

The white muscle that is shown in the center of the scallop is the edible portion.

USING SCALLOP SHELLS AS DISHES

The scallop shell is undoubtedly the world's most prized shell for use as a dish, as well as an unlimited number of other decorative purposes. Food, of any kind, that is cooked or served in a scallop shell can't help but be asthetically attractive.

To prepare scallop shells for use as food containers, they should be thoroughly scrubbed and then boiled for 20 minutes in water containing 1 tablespoon baking soda per quart. After this treatment, scallop shells will be sterile enough to be used in any food preparation, or as serving dishes.

SCALLOP RECIPES

Although we in this country eat only the little white adductor muscle of the scallop, the entire contents of the animal is not only edible but delicious. In Europe, the West Indies, and in South America, the whole animal is used and adored, the usual manner of preparation being to mince the meat with herbs and seasonings and bake the entire scallop in its shell. I know of no shellfish that is more delicious than scallops cooked in this manner. Do try it sometime if you should get the urge to experiment. I don't know what possessed us in North America to fall into the habit of discarding nine-tenths of the scallops' meat, thereby annually wasting hundreds of tons of nourishing and delectable food. It's a mystery to me, and just goes to point out another example of the fact that we are perhaps the most wasteful people in the world.

In the following recipes for scallops, you need only concern yourself with that portion of the scallop normally consumed by we Americans—the tender, white, round adductor muscle.

Baked Scallops

Jim Kerrigan, from Cape Cod, passes along this recipe for baked scallops, which is an easy and tasty dish to prepare. The finished dish gives you a scallop with a crisp brown crust containing tender, white, moist meat within.

24 large scallops, shucked	½ cup melted butter
3 eggs, beaten	½ cup cracker crumbs

Drain and dry the scallops carefully. Dip them in beaten egg, then in cracker crumbs and arrange them in a single layer in a shallow, well-buttered baking pan. Pour a generous amount of melted butter over the top and bake in a very hot oven (425° F.). Turn frequently until well browned on all sides. Serve hot with lemon slices, tartar sauce, or catsup. Oven fried potatoes and a side dish of cole slaw goes well with this dish. Serves 2.

Scallop Stew

½ pound butter	1 quart milk

½ quart scallop meat   1 chopped onion (optional)

Melt the butter in a frying pan and cook the scallops in it just until they turn pure white (5 or 6 minutes). Add scallops and butter, from frying pan, to hot milk which has been preheated in a large saucepan. Serve piping hot with a sprinkle of salt and pepper.

The bigger batch of this stew that you have left over the better. The more times you reheat this and serve it as "leftovers," the better it will taste.

The addition of an onion sauted in butter will give a nice tang to the stew. Serves 6.

The scallop shell used as the emblem of the Shell Oil Company, is a fossil species from California. All of the more than 200 tankers of the Shell Oil fleet are named after the various genera of mollusks. Their first launched ship was christened the S.S. Murex. Aboard each of these vessels, a specimen of the ship's namesake mollusk is mounted in an attractive glass exhibit case.

Pan-Fried Scallops

1 egg, beaten   ½ cup flour
1 tablespoon milk   ½ cup cracker crumbs
1 teaspoon salt and   1 pound Scallops, shucked
  pinch of pepper

Combine egg, milk, and salt and pepper. Combine flour and cracker crumbs. Dip scallops in egg mixture then roll in flour and crumbs.

Place scallops into a frying pan containing about ⅛ inch of hot fat. Fry over a moderate heat until brown on one side, turn gently and brown other side. The cooking time should not exceed more than about 5 minutes. Drain on soft paper towels after frying and serve hot. Serves 2 to 3.

Toasted Scallops

A most delicious way to eat scallops is by toasting them over a bed of hot coals, on the end of a stick, just as you would toast marshmallows. Dip them into cold tartar sauce and eat immediately.

Broiled Scallops

1 pound scallops, shucked   Salt and pepper to taste
¼ cup melted butter or   1 teaspoon lemon juice
   margarine

Preheat oven broiler to 400° F. Spread scallops in a shallow broiling pan, making sure to leave a space between each piece of scallop meat. Pour melted butter over scallops. Sprinkle with salt and pepper. Broil about 3 inches from heat for about 2 minutes; turn, sprinkle with lemon juice, and broil 3 minutes longer, or until tender. Serve with an herb butter. Serves 4.

For herb butter: Combine 1 cup melted butter with ½ teaspoon chive, ½ teaspoon parsley, and ½ teaspoon tarragon.

The earliest known collection of seashells, unearthed from the ruins of Pompeii, contained many scallop shells. It is thought that this collection might have belonged to Pliny who was a distinguished naturalist of the time. Pliny was also the first naturalist to record the swimming activities of the scallop.

Scallop and Radish Soup

½ pound scallops, shucked   ¼ teaspoon oregano
24 radishes   ¼ teaspoon garlic
 1 teaspoon salt   ¼ teaspoon pepper

Wash scallops and peel radishes. Place scallops and radishes into a large saucepan with 7 cups water and cook over a low heat for 10 minutes. Add salt and other seasonings to taste; then continue to cook at a low heat until radishes become tender. Serves 6.

Scallop Cocktail

½ pound scallops, shucked
Lettuce
Cocktail sauce

Boil scallops in salted water for 3 to 5 minutes; then drain. Arrange lettuce in bottom of 4 cocktail glasses, place scallops on top, and cover with cocktail sauce. Serves 4. See Chapter Nine for several ways to prepare cocktail sauce.

Scallop Hors d'Oeuvres

1 pound cooked scallops
¼ cup mayonnaise
1 tablespoon parsley, chopped
1 teaspoon lemon juice

¼ teaspoon salt
¼ teaspoon Worcestershire sauce
1 egg white, beaten
1 dash pepper

To cook scallops, boil in salted water for about 5 minutes.

Mix together all ingredients except scallops and egg white. Then fold this mixture into well beaten egg white. Place scallops on a greased cookie sheet. Top each scallop with first mixture. Place under broiler for about 3 minutes, or until lightly browned. Makes 36.

Cape Cod Scallop Supper

4 medium-sized baking
   potatoes
½ pound cooked scallops
   (boiled 5 minutes)

4 heaping tablespoons butter
4 heaping tablespoons flour
½ teaspoon salt
1 cup milk

½ cup cooked whole kernel corn

Wash and bake potatoes in a hot oven until soft. Cut scallops into halves.

Melt butter and blend into flour and salt. Gradually add milk and cook this mixture until it becomes thick and smooth, stirring constantly. Stir in scallops and corn, heat well, but do not boil. Remove potatoes from oven and slice them open at the tops. Serve the scallop mixture over the tops of hot potatoes. Serves 4.

If you would place a scallop into a jar of sea water and allow it to become relaxed enough to open its shell in the feeding position, you will have a grand opportunity to observe the bright array of blue or emerald-green eyes which dot the inside of the scallops mantle edge. There will be two dozen or more of these eyes on both the upper and lower mantle edges. It is generally supposed that these eyes do not truly see, but can only sense changes in light intensity.

Scallops Baked in the Shell

2 pounds scallops, shucked   1 dash pepper
¼ cup butter   ¼ teaspoon sugar
¼ cup chili sauce   2 cups dry cracker crumbs
½ teaspoon salt   ¼ cup sliced onion

Wash scallops and cut into ½ inch pieces. Combine butter, chili sauce, salt, pepper, sugar, cracker crumbs, and scallops. Place this mixture into greased scallop shells (use the deep shell halves). Place a slice of onion on the top of each and bake at 350° F. for 20 to 25 minutes, or until browned. Serves 6.

Baked Scallops and Tomatoes

2 tomatoes   1 teaspoon celery salt
Salt and pepper to taste   1 teaspoon Worcestershire sauce
1 tablespoon butter   ¼ pound scallops, shucked
                  ½ cup grated cheese (any variety)

Slice tomatoes into 4 pieces and arrange on a well greased, shallow baking pan. Sprinkle each with salt and pepper. Mix together butter, celery salt, and Worcestershire sauce. Dip scallops into butter mixture then place on top of tomatoes. Sprinkle grated cheese over each and bake in a hot oven (400° F) for 15 minutes. Serve piping hot. Serves 2.

Creamed Scallops

2 cups raw scallops, shucked   ½ cup milk
3 tablespoons butter   ½ cup light cream
2 tablespoons flour   1 egg, beaten
                  Salt and pepper to taste

Simmer scallops in boiling salted water until tender (about 5 min.); drain well.

Melt butter in a saucepan and add flour, stirring until smooth. Lower heat and slowly add milk and cream (if desired, you can add either all milk or all cream), stirring constantly until thick and smooth. Stir in the seasonings and scallops; then reduce heat to lowest possible flame and add beaten egg. Simmer and stir the mixture until egg sets (about 2 min.). Serves 4.

This dish is delicious when served over buttered toast.

Skewered Scallops

½ quart raw scallops, shucked
6 thick slices uncooked bacon
1/3 cup melted butter

Cut bacon into 1 inch slices. Place scallops on skewer stick alternately with bacon strips. Brush all with melted butter and broil about 3 inches from flame until bacon is crisp. Serve with cocktail or tartar sauce. Serves 4.

Long Island Scallop Bake

½ cup butter	⅓ cup flour
½ cup onion, chopped	2 cups light cream
1 cup celery, chopped	1 pound raw scallops, shucked
1 cup mushrooms (canned)	1⅔ cups soft bread crumbs
1 cup green pepper, chopped	⅓ cup grated Parmesan cheese

¾ teaspoon salt

Melt 2 tablespoons butter in large frying pan. Saute onions, celery, mushrooms and green pepper until almost tender. Melt ¼ cup butter in large saucepan. Add flour and salt, stirring until mixture is smooth. Gradually add cream and lower heat to the simmering point; cook and stir until thick and smooth. Add vegetable mixture and scallops to sauce and mix well. Place in large casserole dish, top with bread crumbs, grated cheese, and a bit of butter. Bake in a 350° F. oven for 15 to 20 minutes, or until bubbly and browned on top. Serves 6.

Deep-Fried Scallops

½ pound raw scallops, shucked   1 egg, beaten
¼ cup flour   ½ cup fine bread crumbs, dry

Roll scallops in flour then dip each in egg and roll in bread crumbs. Fry in deep, hot fat until browned (about 3 to 5 min.). Serve hot with tartar sauce. Serves 2.

Pineapple Scallops

8 slices pineapple (canned)   1 tablespoon onion, minced

1 pound raw scallops, shucked   1 pinch of salt
⅓ cup butter, melted   ½ teaspoon Worcestershire sauce

Place pineapple slices in bottom of a shallow, well-greased baking dish. Arrange 2 or 3 scallops in the center of each ring.

Combine butter, onion, salt, and Worcestershire. Pour this mixture over pineapple and scallops. Bake in a 400° F. oven for 10 to 15 minutes. Serves 4.

Individual Baked Scallops

1 pound raw scallops, shucked   6 tablespoons heavy cream
Salt and pepper to taste   6 teaspoons dry bread crumbs
4 teaspoons butter, melted

Place equal amounts of scallops in four individual greased baking dishes. Sprinkle with salt and pepper. Add 1½ tablespoons cream to each dish and top with 1½ teaspoons bread crumbs and a teaspoon of melted butter. Bake in a 400° F. oven for about 20 minutes, or until browned on top. Serves 4.

Connecticut Scallop Casserole

1 pound raw scallops, shucked   3 tablespoons flour
1 tablespoon lemon juice   ¾ teaspoon salt
1 dash cayenne pepper   1 cup milk
1 tablespoon onion, minced   2 egg yolks, beaten
¼ teaspoon thyme   3 tablespoons white wine
3 tablespoons butter   ½ cup Cheddar cheese, grated

Place scallops in a large saucepan with 2 cups water, lemon juice, cayenne pepper, onion and thyme. Boil gently for 5 minutes. Drain scallops and save the liquid.

Melt 3 tablespoons butter in saucepan and stir in flour and salt. Gradually add milk, stirring constantly until thick and smooth. Add beaten egg yolks, wine and scallops to the sauce and stir for 2 minutes. Add cheese and stir until completely melted. Pour into casserole dish and bake in a 350° F. oven for 10 minutes. Bread crumbs may be sprinkled over the top prior to baking if you like. Serves 4.

Skillet Scallops

2 pounds scallops, fresh or
frozen
1 package (7 ounces) frozen
pea pods
¼ cup butter or margarine
2 tomatoes, cut into eighths

¼ cup water
2 tablespoons cornstarch
1 tablespoon soy sauce
½ teaspoon salt
⅛ teaspoon pepper
3 cups hot cooked rice

Soy sauce

Thaw frozen scallops and pea pods. Rinse scallops with cold water to remove any shell particles. Cut large scallops in half crosswise. Drain pea pods. Melt butter in a 10-inch fry pan. Add scallops and cook over low heat for 3 to 4 minutes, stirring frequently. Add pea pods and tomatoes. Combine water, cornstarch, soy sauce, salt, and pepper. Add to scallop mixture and cook until thick, stirring constantly. Serve in a rice ring with soy sauce. Makes 6 servings.

Chapter Four

Mussels

ABOUT MUSSELS

MUSSEL, A NAME applied to several common bivalves among which are:
(1) The common sea-mussel (Mytilus edulis), very important as a source of
bait for fishermen and not unfrequently used as food. It is widely distributed in crowded beds between high and low water marks. (2) The horse-
mussel (Modiolus modiola) is nearly twice as large as the above, and lives
a more active burrowing life below the low water mark. (3) The freshwater mussels, Unionidae, are fairly widely distributed in lakes, and rivers
of this country, where they plow their way along the bottom from one
resting place to another. Among the chief representatives of the Unionadae
are, the pond-mussel, the painter's-mussel, and the widely distributed
pearl-mussel.

Mussels are worldwide in distribution and occur in a variety of habitats
ranging from well above the low-tide line to moderate depths below the
low-tide line. The mussel (Myilide) family is an ancient group dating from
at least the Paleozoic era.

The many species of the mussel family are all characterized by inequi-
lateral valves, wedge-shaped or oval, which articulate close to the animals
anterior end. They do possess a foot like the clam family, but this foot is

59

small in relation to the size of the shell. However, their foot is capable of considerable extension.

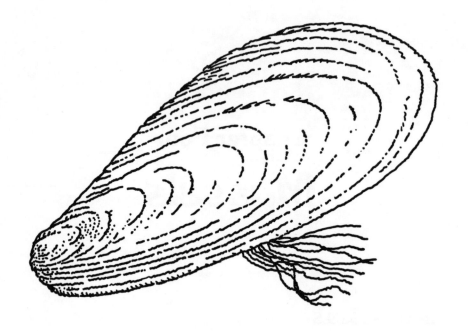

THE COMMON EDIBLE MUSSEL

THE SHELLFISH WITH A BEARD

Mussels live attached to the surface of rocks and pilings, or to shells and other materials embedded in muddy bottoms.

The byssus (beard), a holdfast device by which the shell is attached, is composed of numerous fine but tough threads produced by a gland in their foot. The threads act as effective anchors to secure the mussel against the buffeting of the waves. Once they secure themselves upon an object they are not necessarily there to stay permanently. They can release themselves and move about at will.

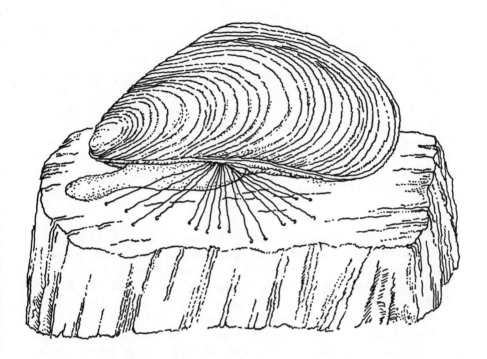

HOW A MUSSEL ATTACHES ITSELF TO ROCKS, ETC. BY
BYSSUS THREADS (BEARD)

GATHERING MUSSELS

Mussels are commonly found clinging to rocks, pilings, edges of
wharves, and even imbedded in hard mud. It is best to pick them at low
tide. At this time the freshest ones will be exposed just at the edge of the
water and will be quite easy to gather. Try to get those which are as close
to the water, or in the water, at low tide. Obviously these will be the best
fed mussels and therefore the plumpest and tenderest of the lot.

Mussels cling to their homes by a beard (byssus), so when you are
picking mussels, be sure there is some resistance and that some portion of
their beard is visible protruding from their shells, this will assure you that
the mussel is alive and healthy.

Dead mussels, which often become filled with mud, are fairly common
in some areas. They are about the same weight as live ones and if the shells

are closed they can easily fool you. If you should unknowingly gather some don't worry because when you throw them into a pot to steam them open, they will remain closed and won't spill out their muddy contents.

There is only one way to gather mussels, and that is to simply pull them off whatever they are attached to by hand. They abound on both coasts of the United States and, as far as I know, there are not presently any laws regarding their taking, nor limits imposed on amounts that may be taken.

On the East coast of the U.S. mussels can be gathered and eaten throughout the year. They are always safe to eat if care is taken not to gather them from polluted areas.

West Coast Caution: On the West coast of the U.S., including Canadian and Alaskan waters, mussels are liable to cause severe stomach upsets if eaten during the warm spring and summer months of May through October. At that time of year they feed on a certain kind of "blooming" plankton which is toxic to humans. To be safe, gather mussels on the west coast from November through April. During these months you will have no problems with eating mussels, and can safely gorge yourself on their delicious contents.

HOW TO OPEN MUSSELS

To begin with, mussels need a good scrubbing with a stiff brush to remove all exterior mud, etc. Next you must pull off that portion of the beard which is still attached to the mussel, and sticking out of the shell. This can be accomplished by simply grasping it between your fingers and giving it a pull outwards, and at the same time, toward the wide end of the shell.

The only practical method of opening mussels is to steam them open. Place them in a large pot or kettle with a tight fitting lid. Place a half cup of water in the bottom and set over low heat until the shells open. After the shells have cooled enough to handle, you can pick out the meat and continue on with your favorite recipe, or just dunk them in melted butter and eat right away. If any shells should remain closed after a few minutes of steaming, discard them. They are most probably full of gooey mud.

If you should want to open raw mussels for any reason, such as to prepare the recipe I have given for Hobo Mussels, simply insert a strong bladed knife between the shells and force them open. It's not at all difficult to open mussels in this manner, but, would be terribly time consuming if, for instance, you were going to open a two gallon pail full, which might contain upwards of 125 mussels.

USING MUSSEL SHELLS AS DISHES

Mussel shells are rather small for ordinary use as dishes, but can prove interesting when both halves of the shell are utilized together. Stuffed with food and tightly closed, the contents will be a surprise to your guests, as will the beautiful mother-of-pearl lining that graces the mussels interior.

Mussel shells should be scrubbed thoroughly and then boiled for 20 minutes in water containing 1 teaspoon of baking soda per quart. After this treatment they are ready to be used for stuffing with food.

MUSSEL RECIPES

Steamed Mussels

24 large mussels, in the shell   ¼ cup dry white wine
¼ cup water   Melted butter

Thoroughly scrub and debeard mussels. Place in a kettle with the water and wine. Cover and steam until shells have opened. Serve with melted butter as a dip. Serves 2.

French Style Steamed Mussels

4 dozen large mussels,   ½ cup water
   in the shell   1 onion, sliced
½ cup wine (red or white)   1 pinch garlic salt

Thoroughly scrub and debeard mussels. Place in a large kettle with wine and water, onion, and garlic salt. Cover tightly and steam for 20 minutes. Remove from heat and pick the meat from the opened mussels, dipping each in melted butter. Gulp down immediately. Serves 4.

The sedentary, bivalve mollusks, such as mussels and oysters, do not expend much energy to obtain their food. It is brought to them by the action of the tides and currents. For this reason, a much higher percentage of food consumed by them is converted into flesh than, for instance, in the case of land animals which must forage for themselves and waste a great portion of their food in the energy expended to move about.

Fried Mussels

2 dozen mussels   Salt and pepper to taste
1 egg   ½ cup flour
1 tablespoon cold water   ½ cup bread crumbs
     1½ cups cooking oil (approximate)

Pry open fresh, cleaned mussels and remove their meat. Beat egg with 1 tablespoon cold water and season with salt and pepper. Sprinkle mussels with flour, then roll in bread crumbs, and dip in egg mixture. Roll again in bread crumbs and allow to stand a few minutes before frying.

Deep fry in hot grease for 3 minutes, or until brown. Drain on paper towels and serve hot with tartar sauce. See sauce chapter in this book for several ways to prepare a tartar sauce. Serves 2.

Creamed Mussels on Toast

2 dozen mussels, in the shell	½ cup milk (or light cream)
½ cup mussel broth	Salt and pepper to taste
1 heaping tablespoon butter	1 teaspoon parsley, chopped
1 heaping tablespoon flour	4 pieces butterd toast

Place mussels in a covered kettle with about ¼ cup water and steam until shells open (be sure they are first thoroughly cleaned). Remove meat from opened shells. Strain broth and set aside ½ cupful of it.

Melt butter, add flour, stir and cook over low heat in a saucepan until smooth. Slowly add the ½ cup of mussel broth and bring to a boil. Add milk, stirring constantly until mixture thickens. Season to taste with salt and pepper. Add mussels and heat through, but do not boil. Serve on buttered toast with a parsley garnish. Serves 2.

In Spain, where mussels are raised commercially by aquaculture methods, the production of mussels is close to 250,000 pounds of meat (not including the shell) per acre. Compare that figure with a maximum of 300 pounds of meat per acre for cattle production and you can visualize the great potentials of farming the sea.

Mussels in Tomato Sauce

2 dozen mussels, in the shell	Salt and pepper to taste
2 cups dry white wine	1 dash of oregano
2 cups water	1 tablespoon butter
½ onion, chopped	4 large tomatoes, peeled and chopped

Wash and debeard mussels. Place in a large kettle with water, onion, wine, and salt and pepper and oregano. Cook until shells open (4 or 5 minutes). Remove mussels from the liquid and take the meat out of the shells. Set aside both for the moment.

Melt butter in a saucepan, then add tomatoes and mussel broth and simmer for 10 minutes, stirring to a pulp. Add mussel meat and simmer an additional 5 minutes before serving. Serves 2.

Hobo Mussels

Hobos and beachcombers often take advantage of the readily available mussel to indulge themselves in an inexpensive meal. It goes like this!

One loaf of bread and one onion are purchased beforehand, then when the mood to eat strikes, a dozen or so raw mussels are gathered and opened. A slice of raw onion is placed on a piece of bread and topped with a raw mussel. The bread is folded in half and all is eaten with much gusto.

Mussel Patties

2 cups cooked mussel meat,   5 eggs
   chopped   Salt and pepper to taste
            1 cup crushed crackers

Mix all ingredients in a bowl with a fork. Do not beat. Form into patties and fry on both sides in hot butter until browned. Turn once to brown on both sides. Serves 2.

It would be best to try a sample pattie first. If it does not hold together, you may need to add more cracker crumbs or another egg. The reason for this is that the firmness of the patties produced by this recipe will vary somewhat with the size of the eggs, amount of moisture in the mussels, or the type of crackers you use (I use saltines).

Mussels Dieppoisé

2 cups mussel meat, cooked
1 cup white sauce

Place freshly steamed mussel meat into serving dishes and pour white sauce over them. Serve hot. Serves 2.

Serve with Medium-thick White Sauce, the recipe for which is given in Chapter Nine.

Mussels Brose

2 cups cooked oatmeal   Salt to taste
½ cup boiling water   Butter
2 dozen mussels, cooked
   and shucked

Combine first 4 ingredients, heat thoroughly, then place in serving bowl. Top with a dab of butter and serve hot. Serves 2.

Mussel Luncheon Dish

4 dozen mussels

½ cup white wine

1 cup water

1 large onion, chopped

¼ cup olive oil

1 diced carrot

1 diced potato

2 cloves garlic

2 teaspoons sugar

1 small can stewed tomatoes, drained

4 tablespoons tomato paste

Salt and pepper to taste

Steam well scrubbed and debearded mussels until shells open in ½ cup water and ½ cup white wine. Remove meat from shells and reserve the cooking liquid. Set both aside for the moment.

Fry onions in olive oil until well done and golden brown. Add carrots, potatoes, garlic cloves, sugar, drained tomatoes, and tomato paste. Season with salt and pepper and moisten with mussel liquid. Simmer over a low heat, stirring gently, until the vegetables are well cooked; add more mussel liquid if necessary. Last, add the mussels and simmer for an additional 5 minutes. Remove from heat and serve hot. Serves 4 to 6 persons.

You will find this dish just as tasty served cold as a leftover dish.

Mussel Omelet

2 quarts fresh mussels, in the shell

5 eggs

Salt and pepper to taste

½ cup parsley, chopped

Steam open mussels and remove their meat. The two quarts of mussels should produce just over a cup of meat. In a bowl, beat eggs, add mussels, salt, pepper, and chopped parsley. Stir well then cook in a frying pan just until egg firms up. Serves 4 to 6.

Mussel Fritters

The tender, pinkish meat of the blue mussel, which has a flavor equally as sweet as the best small clams, makes a wonderful tasting batch of fritters. This recipe may become a habit forming dish.

½ cup mussels, cooked and shucked	1 cup flour
½ cup milk	1 teaspoon melted butter
1 egg	1 teaspoon baking soda
	1 pinch salt
3 tablespoons shortening	

Sift together flour, baking powder, and salt in a large bowl. Beat egg until foamy and add to flour mixture. Blend well. Now add milk and melted butter slowly to the flour mixture and blend until smooth. Add mussel meat to batter and mix well. Serves 2.

Melt shortening (or butter) in frying pan. Drop spoonsful of batter into the hot frying pan and fry until golden brown on both sides. Serve with tartar sauce or any of your favorite sauces.

Chinese Mussel Soup

2 chicken bouillon cubes	3 tablespoons cornstarch
3 tablespoons white vinegar	3 eggs
2 tablespoons soy sauce	Pinch black pepper
1 teaspoon salt	½ pound cooked mussels, shelled

Dissolve bouillon cubes in 1 cup boiling water and add soy sauce and salt. Dissolve cornstarch in 1 cup cold water. Pour both mixtures into saucepan and add 4 cups boiling water. Simmer over low flame for 10 minutes. Beat eggs lightly and slowly add to simmering mixture, stirring constantly. Add vinegar, pepper and mussels and simmer an additional 5 minutes. Serves 6.

Brazilian Mussels

1 tablespoon butter	½ cup celery, chopped
½ cup tomatoes, sliced	1 teaspoon salt
1 green pepper, finely chopped	Pepper to taste
2 tablespoons onion, finely chopped	1 tablespoon Worcestershire sauce
	3 cups steamed mussels, shucked

Mix together all ingredients except mussels and Worcestershire sauce. Simmer in a covered saucepan, with just a bit of hot water if necessary, until vegetables are tender (about 20 min.). When sauce is done, add Worcestershire sauce to it and pour over hot steamed mussels on heated platters. Serves 4.

Cream of Mussel Soup

1 cup cooked mussels, shucked and minced	1 cup milk
	1 tablespoon butter
1 cup cream	Salt and pepper to taste

Heat mussels, cream, and milk in a saucepan but do not allow the mixture to boil. When heated, add butter and seasonings. Serve piping hot, with croutons or crackers. Serves 2 to 3.

Mussels en Brochette

48 large mussels, in the shell	2 lemons, wedged
6 thick slices uncooked bacon	Salt and pepper to taste
6 stuffed green olives	Cocktail sauce

Open raw mussels and remove meat. Trim off all the dark bearded portions; drain. Season mussels with a sprinkling of salt and pepper. Cut slices of bacon into 1 inch pieces. Alternately place mussels and bacon strips on 6 skewer sticks. Center an olive on each stick.

Place skewers on a shallow baking tray and broil for about 2 minutes on each side, or until bacon is crisp. Position skewers about 3 inches from flame.

Serve piping hot with cocktail sauce (see Chapter Nine) and lemon wedges. Serves 6.

Easy Mussel Chowder

2 cups cooked mussels, shucked meat	1 quart milk
	½ cup butter
1½ cups potatoes, diced	1 teaspoon salt
1 onion, thinly sliced	¼ teaspoon pepper

Cook mussels and set liquor aside. Chop with smallish pieces. Cook potatoes and onion in 2 cups of mussel liquor until tender. Heat (but do not boil) milk and add remaining ingredients. Bring completed chowder to the boiling point to heat thoroughly. Serve with crackers floating on top. Serves 4.

As with all chowders, this is even better when heated up the second day.

Mussel Curry

5 tablespoons butter	2 cups milk
1 onion, finely chopped	1 teaspoon curry powder
1 clove garlic, minced	Salt and pepper to taste
3 tablespoons flour	¾ pound cooked mussels, shucked

Melt butter in top of a double boiler over boiling water. Add onion and garlic and cook until tender. Blend in flour and gradually add milk, stirring constantly until thick and smooth. Stir in curry powder, salt and pepper to taste and mussels. Heat through and serve.

This mixture goes well over cooked rice. Serves 6.

Mussel Loaf

1½ cups cooked mussels, shucked	¾ cup milk, scalded
½ cup butter, melted	1 small onion, finely chopped
1½ cups mashed potatoes	3 eggs, beaten
	1 teaspoon salt
½ teaspoon black pepper	

Mix half of the melted butter with all other ingredients except eggs. Next stir eggs thoroughly into the mixture. Place in a well-greased loaf pan and bake for about 35 minutes in a 375° F. oven, or until loaf is firm and browned on top.

Pour remaining melted butter over top of loaf and serve hot. This loaf is equally good served hot or cold. Serves 6.

Chapter Five

Lobsters

ABOUT LOBSTERS

LOBSTER, A SPECIES of crustacean, of the order Decapoda. One of the largest and most valuable of all Crustaceans, being second only to the oyster as an item of food among the marine invertebrates of the North Atlantic coast (our common northern lobster is Homarus americanus).

The claws of a lobster are very powerful and unequal. One claw, usually the left, is thicker, more globose and heavier than the other, the biting-edges being furnished with blunt tubercles of different sizes; the other claw is more slender and elongated, and its biting-edges are furnished with numerous small teeth.

The lobster, like other arthropods, is surrounded by an external skeleton, which is a dead, inelastic product, and therefore must be periodically cast off in order to allow the lobster to further grow. The frequency of this molting depends upon the age and nutrition of the animal, and is the register of its growth. During the first four months of its life, the lobster molts from eight to ten times, the adult female probably not more than once in two years, and the giant lobsters, weighing upwards of 20 pounds, at much longer intervals. Hard-shelled lobsters have the finest flesh, stand up well to transportation, and therefore are the most valuable for the commercial

71

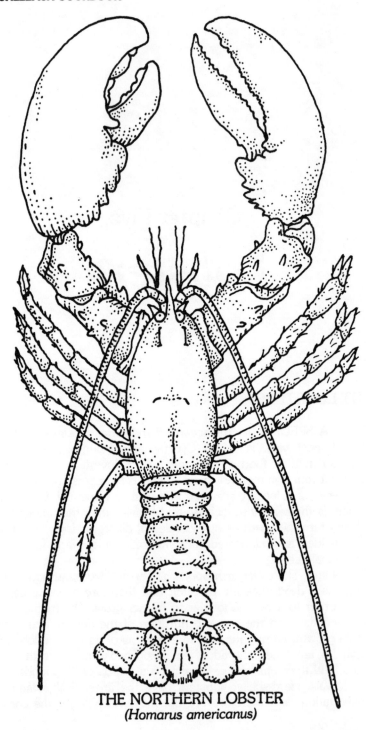

THE NORTHERN LOBSTER
(Homarus americanus)

market. A larger proportion of lobsters taken in the fall, winter and early spring are of this variety.

The color of lobsters during life is usually bluish-black or greenish-black and only changes to red upon boiling. The lobster never swims at the surface of the water, but crawls or walks on the tips of its legs. By use of its flexible tail section, it is capable of darting backwards with astounding speed, sometimes covering 25 feet in less than a second. Lobsters are scavengers and mainly subsist on fish, shell-fish, and other forms of animal matter, both dead and alive.

The lobster is a sedentary animal, its only migrations being to and from deep water. In spring (about April and May) they move toward shore, and in fall (October and November) they again move back to deeper water.

The extreme northern limits of the North American lobster seem to be at around the Straits of Belle Isle. The Canadian Maritime Provinces and the State of Maine constitute the greatest lobster producing territory of the Atlantic Coast. However, lobster production on a commercial basis extends southward to New Jersey.

THE SPINY LOBSTER

As the name may indicate, spiny lobsters received their name on account of the numerous spines located on their legs and body. However, they lack the large claws of the northern lobster: their meat is contained almost entirely in their large, broad tails.

Spiny lobsters are native to the Southern Atlantic states and the Southern California coast. Their meat is about equal in taste and quality to the northern lobster, and can be cooked and eaten in the very same ways. Live spiny lobsters are available on the market in some parts of Florida and California. They should be alive at the time of cooking as should the northern lobster. When the spiny is cooked, its shell turns from brownish-green to "lobster-red," and the meat has the same snowy white color tinged with red that the meat of the northern lobster has.

Laws presently affecting the taking of spiny lobsters are not as strict as for the northern lobster. However, this variety of lobster is fast becoming a popular food item and stricter laws are sure to follow. The spiny lobster is world wide in distribution, ranging through temperate, sub-tropical, and tropical waters of the Atlantic, Pacific, and Indian Oceans.

BUYING LOBSTERS

When purchasing live lobsters, try to avoid buying them out of a tank if possible but rather from a fish market where they keep them on crushed

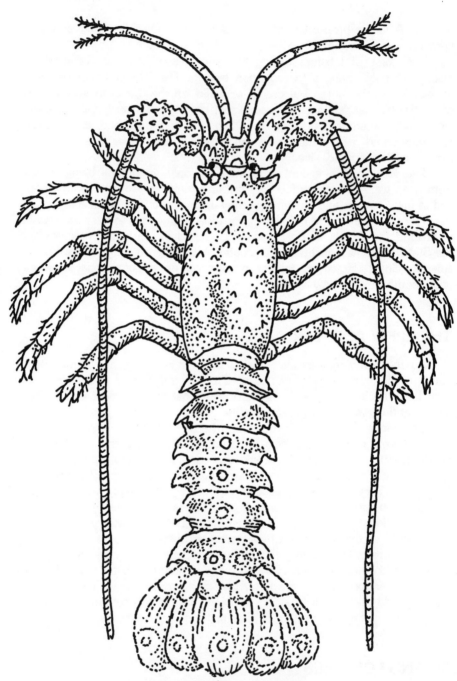

THE SPINY LOBSTER
EAST COAST VARIETY - *Panulirus argus*
WEST COAST VARIETY - *Panulirus interruptus*

ice; lobsters kept in tanks always contain two or three ounces of water which can be mighty expensive at today's high prices. The legs of lobsters sold as "live" should show signs of movement and when picked up, its tail should curl up underneath its body. You may store live lobsters in the coldest part of your refrigerator for a few hours, but don't chance it longer than that. Eat them the same day that you buy them. Never try to keep them fresh by placing them into salted water; the salt content will be all wrong and the water probably not cold enough.

Whole lobsters, cooked in the shell, are also available in most fish markets. They should be bright red in color and have a fresh "seashore" odor to them. The tail of a cooked lobster should spring back to the curled position quickly after it has been straightened out.

CATCHING LOBSTERS

Unfortunately, there are strictly enforced laws against catching the northern lobster by any means, or for any purpose, by anyone other than a duly licensed and permanent resident of the state in which the lobsters are found. Such persons must follow rigid rules, laid down for the protection of these fast disappearing delicacies of the sea.

If you are in the circumstance where lobstering is available to you as a sport or pastime, all you will need to supply your table with lobster meat is a license and the proper equipment for catching lobsters.

The most commonly used procedure for trapping lobsters is a trap baited with fish or other meat scraps. This trap is dropped to the bottom and checked once a day or so for results. Some good places to set a box trap are around an old wharf or near a rocky area which affords lobsters some hiding places and shelter. If you find the right spot for your trap you are pretty sure to catch a legal sized lobster or two with fairly regular frequency.

Spiny lobsters can be caught by much the same methods as used by northern lobstermen.

Another method, which I have employed successfully for both northern and spiny lobsters, is often used by part time crab fishermen, although a great deal of patience is required to be successful. For this method you first need a large diameter (18 inches to 2 feet) ring with loose netting across it (see illustration). This ring is baited in the center and lowered over the side of a wharf or other area in which you expect to find lobsters. If lobsters are indeed feeding in the area, the chances are good that they will crawl into the netted ring to investigate the bait. A periodical pulling of the net may reward you with a lobster, or perhaps even a crab. When pulling up the net, you must pull fast and furiously or your prey might get its wits together and escape. Give this method a try, and if you have the patience, you will be surprised at the results.

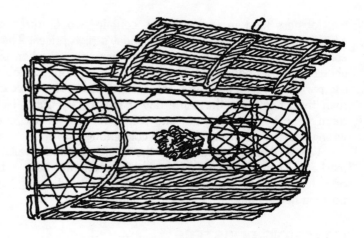

STANDARD LOBSTER TRAP

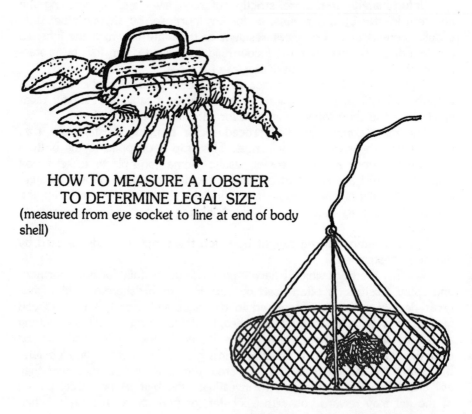

HOW TO MEASURE A LOBSTER
TO DETERMINE LEGAL SIZE
(measured from eye socket to line at end of body
shell)

HOOP NET TRAP WITH BAIT
IN CENTER AND LINE TO SURFACE

COOKING LOBSTERS HUMANELY

Lobsters should always be cooked as soon as possible after being caught or bought. In inland areas of this country people seem to prefer their lobsters broiled, which, I am afraid, usually results in a rather dried-out dish at best. The best way to cook lobster is to boil or steam them by dropping them live into boiling water. It is with this method that many people find themselves struggling with their conscience.

A group of Canadian biologists have determined that lobsters feel no pain at all when dropped live into a pot of boiling water. The reason, they say, is because the lobster lacks the necessary nervous-system equipment. However, if boiling alive still seems a bit brutal to you, follow the advice of the Massachusetts Society for the Prevention of Cruelty to Animals: "Soak the Crustacean first in a mixture of two quarts of cold water to one pound of salt; this "anesthetizes" the lobster so he can be boiled within five minutes without visible signs of discomfort."

The objections to dropping live lobsters into boiling water do not come wholly from those who hold the lobsters feelings within their tender hearts. Some cooks claim it makes the lobster undergo a reflex action which stiffens the muscles and renders the meat much tougher than it should be. Some methods used to overcome this theory and produce a more tender cooked lobster are as follows: (1) Place the lobsters into salt water in a covered pot, turn up the heat until the water reaches a rolling boil and maintain the rolling boil for 10 to 12 minutes, regardless of the lobster's size. (2) Plunge the lobster headfirst into boiling salted water (one table-spoon to a quart), cover the pot and bring the water to the simmering point. Allow the lobsters to simmer for exactly five minutes, plus one minute additional for each quarter-pound over the first pound. (3) Place the lobster into cold salted water (same ratio as above) and then immediately place the pot over high heat on top of the stove. When the lobster is red, it is dead and should immediately be plunged into cold water for a few seconds and then served. This last method was developed by some researchers at Cornell University who claim that it lulls the lobsters gradually to sleep so that they "depart from this word in a drowsy state of euphoria."

HOW TO PREPARE AND EAT A WHOLE BOILED LOBSTER

Remove the lobster from the hot water with tongs. Cool enough to handle. You are then ready to proceed with the preparations for serving. To do this, twist off the large claws and the eight small claws. Then turn the lobster over on its back and with a very sharp knife make a deep incision down the entire length of the lobster and gently force the two halves apart with your fingers. Remove the intestinal vein which runs the length of the tail through the middle of the meat. Remove and discard the stomach, which is a small, hard sack found near the head. Also remove and discard the spongy lungs, which cling to the sides of the body portion of the lobster. The green liver (tomally) and bright red coral (roe—found only in female lobsters) are delicious and considered delicacies. They may be mixed with a little melted butter or mayonnaise and spread on bread or crackers. Arrange all the edible parts of the lobster on a platter and serve with melted butter as a dip.

To eat a lobster, you will need a nutcracker to break the shells of the big claws. Tender and tasty chunks of meat are inside these. Each little claw contains a sweet little morsel that can usually be sucked out. The tail meat is generally considered the best part, and is the most plentiful portion of the lobster. A final search of your lobster will turn up tidbits in the body of the shell, and all of it is good to the last bite. Allow 1 small or ½ large lobster (about 1 pound) per person.

Live lobsters found on today's market usually weigh from 1 to 3 pounds. They are graded in four sizes: Chickens, ¾ to 1 pound; Quarters, 1½ pounds; Large, 1½ to 2½ pounds; and Jumbos, over 2½ pounds.

CLEANING A LOBSTER THE MAINE WAY

The following illustrations describe the Maine way of dealing with a whole boiled lobster. As you can see, the chief instrument used is the hands. "Down Easters" think pretty highly of this method, and as far as I am concerned they must know what they are about. After all, the folks in Maine have been practicing a lot longer than almost anyone else.

Having removed the lobster from the pot, allow to cool down enough to permit handling, and follow the next six steps:

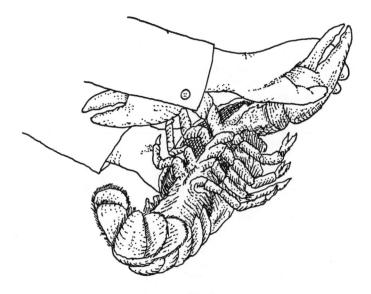

FIGURE 1.

Twist off the large front claws where they join the lobster's body.

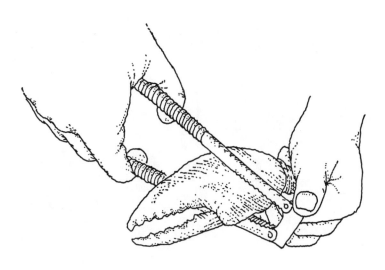

FIGURE 2.

Crack the claws with a nutcracker or light blow from a hammer.

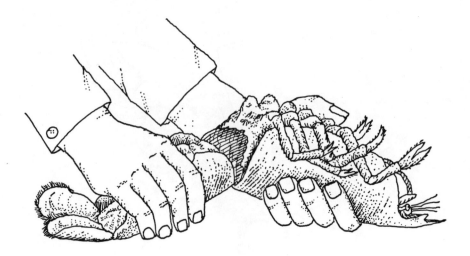

FIGURE 3.

Remove tail from body section by arching the back and twisting until it separates.

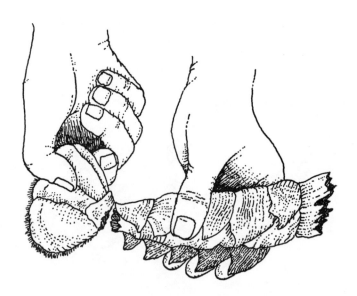

FIGURE 4.

Remove the flippers on the end of the tail by bending backwards until it snaps off.

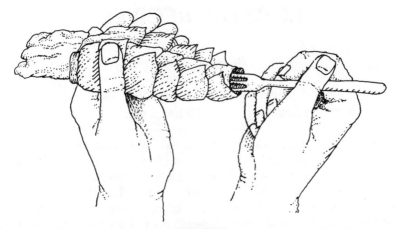

FIGURE 5.

By poking a fork into the hole where the flippers were removed, the entire piece of tail meat may be removed in one simple operation. Just force it out the big end of the tail section.

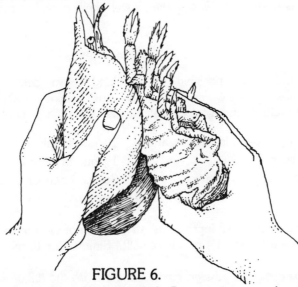

FIGURE 6.

Lift out the back meat from the body shell. Be sure to save the delicious green liver or "tomalley". Pick out the body meat and remove the small legs. The small legs each contain a sweet piece of meat which may be removed by sucking on them like soda straws.

Incidently, this step neatly accomplishes the removal of all inedible body organs. They will .main behind with the head and eyes when you unhinge the back meat and pull it away from the shell.

LOBSTER RECIPES

Boiled Lobster

2 live lobsters (1 pound each)   3 tablespoons salt
3 quarts boiling water   Melted butter

Plunge the lobsters headfirst into salted, boiling water. Cover and boil for 15 minutes. Drain and place lobsters on platters prepared for eating. Serve with melted butter as a dip for the meat. Serves 2.

In recipes calling for cooked lobster meat, follow this method of boiling lobsters, then pick out the meat and proceed with your recipe. Two live lobsters weighing 1 pound each will yield about ½ pound of cooked lobster meat.

If you would like to be fancy when serving boiled lobsters in their shells, rub the shells with olive oil just prior to serving. This treatment will give the lobster shells a perfect appearance.

Lobster Stew

Could there possibly be anything more delicious than a good rich lobster stew served with crisp pilot crackers or toasted English muffins, and a tossed salad as an accompaniment?

1 cup cooked lobster meat,   1½ quarts milk
   diced   1½ quarts cream
4 tablespoons butter   Salt and pepper to taste
          1 dash sherry

Mix together all ingredients. (If you do not wish to use cream, you may substitute a second 1½ quarts of milk.) Simmer for 15 minutes. Serves 2.

The eggs of a lobster, carried underneath the tail of the female, are usually of a dark-green color, spherical, and measure about 1/16th of an inch in diameter. The number of eggs varies with the size of the female that produces them—usually somewhere between 3,000 and 80,000. Female lobsters bearing eggs are always supposed to be thrown back into the sea by any fisherman who catches one in his trap.

Quick Lobster Bisque

The following is a recipe for a very quick lobster bisque that is very good topped with crutons or crumbled up potato chips. Shrimp or crab meat could be used with this recipe instead of lobster with equally as good results.

1 can concentrated	½ teaspoon salt
cream of tomato soup	1 dash pepper
1 can concentrated tomato soup	¼ cup sour cream
1½ cups water	1 cup lobster meat,
1½ teaspoons lemon juice	cooked and diced
Croutons or potato chips	

Combine soups in the top of a double boiler, over boiling water. Add water, lemon juice, salt, and pepper and heat thoroughly. Just before serving, stir in the sour cream and lobster meat. Heat the completed mixture thoroughly and add seasonings. You might like to add a dash of sherry to this dish. Serve as hot as possible, with croutons or crushed potato chips sprinkled on the top. Serves 4 to 6.

Grilled Lobster

2 medium sized live lobsters
Cooking oil
Butter

Place lobsters on their backs and pierce with a sharp knife between the body and tail sections. This will sever the spinal cord, killing them instantly. They never feel a thing, and I hold with this method as the best and most humane way to kill a lobster prior to either boiling or broiling as in this case.

Place lobsters on their backs and slice them open from head to tail, the long way, with a sharp knife. Be careful not to cut all the way through the back shell. Spread the lobsters open and remove the stomach (located near the head) and the black vein which runs from the stomach to the end of the tail. Crack the large claws slightly. Place lobsters in broiler, shell side down, on a shallow baking sheet. Brush with oil or butter, and broil for about 15 minutes, or until slightly browned. Serve with a bowl of melted butter as a dip. Serves 2.

Lobster Newburg

2 tablespoons butter

2 tablespoons flour

¼ teaspoon mustard powder

½ teaspoon salt

Pepper to taste

2 cups light cream

2 well beaten eggs

1 teaspoon brandy

2 tablespoons dry sherry

2 cups lobster meat, cooked

Melt the butter in a saucepan and stir in flour, mustard, salt, and pepper and cook for 3 minutes. Stir in the cream, eggs, brandy, and sherry in that order to complete the Newburg sauce. Add 2 cups of cooked lobster meat to the sauce. Place into individual baking dishes and bake at 325° F. for 15 minutes. Serves 3.

The adult lobster, despite its hard shell, often falls prey to fish of many kinds; among them are the pollock, bass, tautog, shark, and the rays and skates. With the possible exception of man, the cod and striped bass are perhaps the most formidable enemies of the lobster, especially when it is young, or in a soft-shelled condition prior to gaining a new shell after molting.

Lobster Mousse

1 pound lobster meat,
   cooked and chopped

Salt and pepper to taste

¾ cut heavy cream

2 egg whites, beaten

Chop lobster meat into very small pieces; add salt and pepper to taste; beat in heavy cream gradually. Fold in stiffly beaten egg whites and fold the mixture into a mold. Put mold into a pan of hot water and bake at 350° F. for 20 minutes. Unmold the mousse onto a platter and garnish with lemon wedges and parsley. Serve with Hollandaise or lemon sauce over the top. See Chapter Nine for the preparation of either of these sauces. Serves 2.

At the root of the steadily increasing price of shellfish is the mounting price of labor, as well as the growing scarcity of the shellfish themselves. The tending of lobster and crab traps, and the myriad of other tough jobs that go along with the shell-fishing business, are all plain old hard work. They are also jobs that no machine can yet do as well as a man can; and it seems that good men, strong enough to hold up in the tough business of shellfishing, are getting mighty scarce. With these facts in mind, it seems that shellfish prices will continue to climb.

Long Island Lobster Cocktail

2 cups lobster meat, cooked	1 tablespoon lemon juice
½ cup mayonnaise	1 tablespoon parsley, chopped
1 tablespoon catsup	2 teaspoons onion, chopped
Salt and pepper to taste	3 tablespoons white wine

1 dash paprika

Cut lobster meat into medium-sized chunks; mix with the mayonnaise and let cool in the refrigerator for 1 hour. Then add the remaining ingredients, pouring the wine on last. Place into six chilled cocktail glasses and dust with a little paprika. Serves 6.

Quick Lobster Supreme

1 can condensed Cream-of- Asparagus soup	1 cup light cream
	½ pound lobster meat, cooked

3 tablespoons sherry (optional)

Combine all the ingredients and heat to the boiling point. Add sherry, if you like, and serve piping hot. Serves 2 to 3.

Very few lobsters (Homarus americanus) ever reach their potential size in these days of extensive commercial fishing for their kind. If left undisturbed, they have the potential of living upwards of fifty years and approaching fifty pounds in weight.

Baked Stuffed Lobster

2 live lobsters, 1 pound each	2 tablespoons butter, melted
2 cups large bread crumbs, soft	1 tablespoon onion, finely chopped

1 dash garlic salt

Place lobsters on their backs; insert a sharp knife between body and tail section, cutting downward so as to sever the spinal cord. With lobsters on their backs, cut them in half the long way, but not entirely through the top of the shell. Remove the stomach (just in back of the head), and the vein which runs from the stomach to the tip of the tail. Remove and save the green liver and coral roe, if any. Crack the claws slightly.

Combine soft bread crumbs, butter, onion, garlic salt, green liver (tomally), and coral roe. Place this stuffing into the body cavity and over the surface of the tail meat. Place in a shallow baking pan and bake in a hot oven (400° F.) for 20 minutes, or until lightly browned. Serve hot with a bit of melted butter poured over the top if you like. Serves 2.

Baked Stuffed Lobsters with Cheese

2 live lobsters, 1 pound each
1½ cups large, soft bread
   crumbs

2 tablespoons butter, melted
½ cup grated Parmesan cheese
1 dash paprika

Prepare the lobsters in the same way as for plain stuffed lobster in the preceding recipe.

Combine bread crumbs, butter, cheese, green liver, and coral roe. Place this stuffing into the body cavity and over the surface of the tail meat. Sprinkle with paprika. Place in a shallow baking dish and bake at 400° F. for 20 minutes, or until lightly browned. Serve hot with some melted butter over the top. Serves 2.

Lobster Butter

½ cup lobster meat
2 tablespoons butter
Chopped parsley for garnish

Pound lobster meat into a smooth paste. Blend in butter. Place in a dish and top with chopped parsley. Serve with triangles of hot buttered toast or as a spread for crackers. It's delicious! Makes approximately ½ cup.

Lobster Ragout

½ pound lobster meat, cooked
1 pinch black pepper

2 tablespoons butter
¼ teaspoon salt

2 tablespoons cream   1 teaspoon vinegar

Buttered toast

Mix together the lobster meat, pepper, cream, vinegar, and salt.

Melt butter in a saucepan and add the lobster mixture; cook until thoroughly heated through. Serve over buttered toast. Serves 2.

Tart Lobster Salad

1 grapefruit   1 teaspoon grapefruit juice
1 cup lobster meat, cooked   ¼ cup catsup
                  ¼ cup mayonnaise

Cut the grapefruit into small sections and combine with lobster meat. Serve on a bed of lettuce. To make the sauce topping, mix together the grapefruit juice, catsup, and mayonnaise. Serves 2.

Because of its high market value, and the fact that it feeds readily in captivity, the lobster has excited the interest of prospective sea farmers. In fact, adult lobsters have been successfully mated at the Massachusetts State Lobster Hatchery on Martha's Vineyard, and juvenile lobsters have been raised to marketable size in this hatchery.

However, even if it proves economically feasible to feed large numbers of lobsters in captivity, the lobster farmer would be faced with another serious problem: Cannibalism. Lobsters are terribly aggressive toward each other, and are particularly vulnerable to each other immediately after molting. To solve this problem, lobsters must be kept in isolation for five years to reach marketable size. This problem, along with maintenance and feeding, makes lobster farming appear still somewhat impractical at this time.

Lobster Casserole

¼ cup butter   5 cups light cream
¼ cup flour   2 pounds cooked lobster,
2 teaspoons salt   chunks
1 teaspoon Worcestershire   1 package (12 ounces)
  sauce   cooked macaroni

Melt butter in a saucepan and add flour, stirring until a smooth paste is formed. Add remaining ingredients except for macaroni and lobster meat. Simmer slowly (do not boil), stirring constantly until mixture becomes thick and smooth. Remove from heat and add lobster chunks and cooked macaroni. Place in a well-greased casserole dish and bake in a 350° F. oven for about 30 min.

Use a topping of bread crumbs on this casserole if you like. Serves 6.

Lobster Macaroni Salad

½ pound cooked elbow
    macaroni
½ cup mayonnaise
½ cup milk
½ cup French dressing

¾ cup celery, diced
1 small onion, chopped
1 green pepper, chopped
2½ cups cooked lobster meat,
    shredded

Cook macaroni and drain well; chill in refrigerator. Combine mayonnaise, milk and French dressing and mix in with chilled macaroni. Add celery, onion, green pepper and lobster meat; toss well. Serve on a bed of lettuce. Serves 4.

Lobster Chowder

2 cups potatoes, diced
1 cup celery, diced
3 cups water
1 cup creamed corn

2 cups cooked lobster meat
3 tablespoons butter
2 cups milk
1 teaspoon salt and dash pepper

Cook potatoes and celery in 3 cups boiling salted water until tender. Add corn, lobster, butter, milk and seasonings. Simmer gently over low heat (do not boil) for 15 minutes. Serve hot with crackers floating on top. Serves 2 to 6.

Butter-Fried Lobster

¼ cup butter
1 pound lobster meat, cooked
¼ teaspoon oregano

¼ teaspoon thyme
3 tablespoons white wine
Salt and pepper to taste

Melt butter in frying pan; add seasonings and lobster chunks. Cover and allow lobster meat to heat through (about 5 min.). Remove cover and continue to fry for about another 5 minutes, or until browned on all sides.

Lift lobster meat from frying pan and place on heated platters. Immediately add wine to hot butter in frying pan and bring to a boil for 1 minute; then pour over lobster meat and serve piping hot. Serves 4.

Lobster Loaf

1 pound cooked lobster meat, chopped
1 cup soft bread crumbs
½ cup light cream
1 egg, lightly beaten
½ pound Cheddar cheese, sliced
1 tablespoon pimento
Salt and pepper to taste

Combine lobster, bread crumbs, cream, egg and salt and pepper to taste. Place half of this mixture into a 3 inch deep well-greased loaf pan. Cover with a layer of cheese slices, then top with remaining mixture.

Bake in a 375° F. oven for 20 minutes; then top with another layer of cheese slices and garnish with pimentos. Bake another 15 or 20 minutes, or until loaf is firm and cheese is browned. Serves 6.

Chapter Six

Shrimp

ABOUT SHRIMP

THE SHRIMP is a crustaceans belonging to the zoological order of Decapoda. Also classed within this same order are lobsters, crayfish and prawns. The shrimps' form is elongated, tapering, and arched in a hunch-backed shape. The beak portion is very short, which distinguishes it from the prawn. The claws are very small. The entire structure of the shrimp is most delicate, and almost translucent. Its colors are such that the shrimp can readily escape detection by its enemies whether resting on the ocean bottom or swimming through the water. Short, quick darting movements, like short hops, betray their presence to anyone looking attentively into a tide pool left behind by a retiring tide on a sandy shore. When alarmed, the shrimp is capable of burying itself swiftly in the sand by a peculiar movement of its fan-like tail.

From head to tail, the common shrimp can be described thus: The head bears stalked eyes and a set of long feelers behind which lies the thoracic, or forward part of the body, enclosed along the side by a fragile shell, or carapace. The thorax bears five pairs of slender walking legs. The rear portion of the body forms the jointed abdomen, which terminates in the fan-shaped tail, employed by the shrimp in its powerful swimming back-stroke. On its underside, the abdomen section bears well developed swimming paddles (pleopods) to which the female attaches her eggs during the breeding season.

Although many species of shrimp are quite small—some even micro-scopic—a few species reach lengths of eight or more inches. Several hundred different species of shrimp abound in the oceans of the world, but we will concentrate here mainly on the two species found in our own waters. One is the Penacus, found in southern waters from North Carolina to Texas; the other is the Pandalus, found on the Pacific coast from Northern California to Alaska. In these areas shrimp live in the shallow coastal waters, and are available to the patient sportsman who wishes to catch his own supply of fresh shrimp.

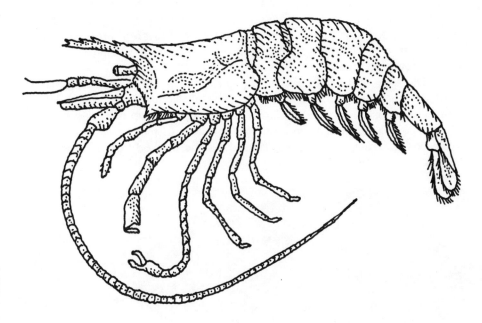

CATCHING SHRIMP

Although it is possible to buy fresh frozen shrimp in almost any food store in the U.S., you can, in certain areas, catch your own supply of fresh shrimp right from the sea.

Shrimp are caught in a variety of ways—with hand casting nets, long seins, baited traps, channel nets set in tideways and channels, and with large boat-drawn otter and beam trawls. For our purposes though, we are most interested in the hand casting net as a method of catching supplies of fresh live shrimp.

This type of net (see illustration) is cast a short distance into the water in a manner that will make it land flat on the waters surface like a giant pancake. Small weights, attached around the outside rim of the nets allow it to sink to the bottom thus trapping everything lying under it. It does not take much practice to become efficient with this type of net, and after a few casts you will get the knack of it. Once the net has settled to the bottom, it is drawn back to the thrower by a long line. Acting like a giant underwater parachute, it will also trap anything that gets in its way while being hauled in. After being drawn in, the net is cleared of its contents. The process is continued until you have caught the desired amount of shrimp.

This hand casting net method is the most effective way I know of to catch your own shrimp supply, and commonly used in the Southern sections of the U.S. As with other types of fishing, don't allow yourself to become easily disappointed. You may have to try several different areas, and make many net casts before you finally locate a school of feeding shrimp in a good shrimping area.

The best shrimping areas of the U.S. for the hand net fishing method are the shallow waters of bays and inlets all along the Southern Atlantic and Gulf coasts from North Carolina to Texas. Shrimp may also be found extending, although sparsley, into fresh waters of most areas. On the Pacific coast, shrimp may be caught by the same method from Northern California all the way up to Alaska.

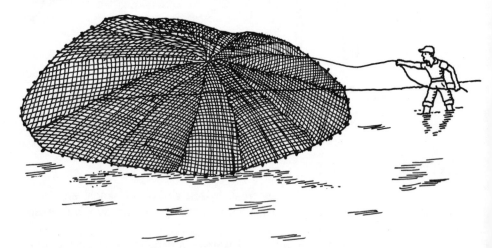

HOW TO CLEAN AND PREPARE SHRIMP

Fresh shrimp are generally marketed either chilled on ice or frozen. Fresh shrimp have usually had the heads and upper body portion (thorax) removed and only need to be thoroughly washed, peeled and deveined prior to use. Shrimps may be peeled either before or after cooking. Both methods will be described here. When preparing dishes calling for pre-cooked shrimp, it is sometimes best to peel them prior to cooking so as to preserve the sweetest flavor and the juiciest meat.

To cook shrimp before shelling, wash thoroughly and place in a sufficient amount of boiling salted water to cover. Use plenty of salt for this method—3 tablespoons salt to each quart of water used should be just about right. Cover the cooking pot and bring the water back to the simmering point (never boil shrimp). Simmer for 3 to 5 minutes, or until the shells just turn pink. Drain and peel shells from the cooked shrimp. Lastly, make a lengthwise cut down the back of each shrimp and remove the black vein that runs down the center of the shrimps tail. Rinse under cold water and chill in the refrigerator. The shrimp are now pre-cooked and ready for use.

To cook shrimp after shelling them in the raw state, wash thoroughly under cold running water and remove the shells with a sharp knife. Make a lengthwise cut down the back of each shrimp and remove the gritty black vein and rinse again in cold water. Place shrimp in enough boiling salted water to cover (with this method less salt is required—1 tablespoon per quart is sufficient). Cover pot and bring the water back to the simmering point for about 3 or 4 minutes, or until the meat turns pinkish. Remove the shrimp from the pot and store in the refrigerator if it is not to be eaten immediately. Strain the broth from the cooking pot through several layers of cheesecloth to trap any remaining sand or grit that may have strayed into the pot. The broth from peeled and cooked shrimp can be used as a substitute for part of the juice in many sauces and soups; the liquor from canned shrimp may also be used in the same way.

As with all shellfish, overcooking will make shrimp tough. The perfect shrimp should be tender and pink colored. To some degree the size of a shrimp will determine the length of time they should be cooked. Just a few minutes cooking is needed for small shrimp, while 10 to 15 minutes are required for large and jumbo sizes.

Incidentally, the deveining process is a long and tedious one and is only necessary on larger shrimp with a dark colored, prominent vein showing. Smaller shrimp really do not require deveining, so save yourself the work when you can. The veins are quite harmless and the main objection to them is the amount of gritty material they contain.

BUYING SHRIMP

Shrimp are marketed fresh and whole, fresh and headless, *frozen, frozen and breaded, canned, and cooked-and-peeled. The most popular of all commercial methods of shrimp preparation is the fresh frozen state. Any frozen shrimp that you buy in the supermarket should be quite good if used within a fairly short period after purchase. As with all shellfish, shrimp will slowly deteriorate in flavor and quality if stored frozen for prolonged periods of time.

All frozen shrimp have usually had the heads removed, but most packing houses leave the outside shell on the shrimp. This shell is easily peeled away either before or after cooking, depending on the recipe and cooking method.

Fresh shrimp should have a fairly mild odor and firm flesh. The color of the shell may range from pinkish to tan or grayish-green.

The standard classes of shrimp in the shell and the number of shrimp in each pound are:

Jumbo	Less than 15 per pound
Extra large	15 to 20 per pound
Large	21 to 25 per pound
Medium	26 to 30 per pound
Small	31 or more per pound

When buying frozen shrimp, select only those packages that are firm and hard, and are stored in a chest at a temperature of zero degrees or colder. Select only undamaged packages, and shy away from torn packages or ones with a queer smell.

Use fresh shrimp within a day or so after purchase. If you must hold them for a short period, store them in a tightly covered container in the coldest part of the refrigerator. Cooked shrimp are highly perishable and will deteriorate very quickly if not refrigerated.

SHRIMP RECIPES

Basic Boiled Shrimp

2 pounds raw shrimp, unpeeled
2 tablespoons salt

Boil thoroughly washed whole shrimp in salted water until pink and tender (5 to 10 minutes). Remove from water and serve immediately, allowing each person to peel his own serving of shrimp. Serve with cocktail sauce (given in the sauce chapter of this book). Serves 2 to 4 persons.

For a variation in flavor, the shrimp may be boiled in water to which wine, sliced lemon, onion, garlic, or other seasonings are added.

Shrimp Creole

2 tablespoons butter	1 small can tomato paste
1 cup onion, chopped	1 pound raw shrimp
½ cup green pepper, chopped	1 teaspoon salt
½ clove garlic, chopped	1 dash pepper

Peel shrimp and wash thoroughly. Remove sand veins from shrimp if large and black. Fry onion, green pepper, and garlic in butter until tender. Add tomato paste, shrimp and seasonings and simmer very gently for about 10 minutes, or until shrimp are tender. Serves 2 to 4.

Shrimp Newburg

¼ cup butter	1½ cups light cream
2 tablespoons flour	2 egg yolks, beaten
½ teaspoon salt	1 pound precooked shrimp,
1 dash cayenne pepper	peeled
1 dash cinnamon	2 tablespoons dry white wine
Toast squares	

Melt butter in a saucepan and gradually blend in the flour and seasonings. Add cream slowly and cook until thick and smooth, stirring constantly. Add a bit of the sauce to the egg yolks and stir; then pour the eggs into the sauce mixture, stirring constantly. Add shrimp meat cut up into small pieces and heat through. Remove from heat and stir in the wine. Serve immediately on toast squares. Serves 6 persons.

Lobster and crabmeat may often be successfully substituted for shrimp in many recipes with   excellent results. You will find that many shellfish recipes are interchangeable; for example, clams may often be used instead of oysters or mussels in a recipe, etc., etc. Use your own imagination to create new and varied shellfish dishes.

Shrimp Casserole

2 pounds raw shrimp, peeled and deveined	¾ pound cooked asparagus tips
5 tablespoons butter	3 tablespoons flour
2 teaspoons salt	2 cups milk
1½ cups Cheddar cheese	2 tomatoes

Pepper to taste

Saute the shrimp in butter and 1 teaspoon of salt for about 5 minutes; then remove from pan and set aside for the moment. To the butter in the pan, add flour, remaining salt, dash pepper and milk, stirring constantly until thickened. Add 1 cup of the cheese and stir until melted. Place asparagus in the bottom of a greased baking dish. Add shrimp, sauce, remaining cheese and top with sliced tomatoes. Broil until cheese turns a golden brown. Serves 6.

Shrimp Bora Bora

1 quart water	½ teaspoon dry mustard
1 cup fresh celery leaves	½ teaspoon black pepper
1 bay leaf	½ teaspoon garlic salt

2 pounds uncooked shrimp (peeled)

Simmer the above ingredients for 20 minutes then add 2 pounds of shrimp. Simmer (do not boil) for an additional 5 minutes, or until shrimp meat turns pink and tender. Use the Dip for Shrimp recipe given in Chapter Nine to prepare the dip to be served with Shrimp Bora Bora. Serves 4 to 6 persons.

Shrimp and Artichoke Hearts

1 package (15 ounces)
frozen artichoke hearts
1 pound cooked shrimp,
peeled
1 tablespoon Worcestershire
sauce

1 small can mushrooms
¼ cup dry sherry
1 cup White Sauce
(See Chapter Nine)
2 tablespoons butter
¼ cup grated Parmesan
cheese

Arrange thawed artichoke hearts in the bottom of a greased baking dish and spread the cooked shrimp over the top of them. Mix Worcestershire sauce, mushrooms and sherry with the white sauce and pour over the top of the shrimp and artichokes in the baking dish. Sprinkle the top with grated cheese and bake for 20 minutes in a 350° F. oven. Serve as hot as possible. Serves 4.

Dr. Frederick J. Stare of the Harvard University Dept. of Nutrition states, "Fish be included in the diet four times a week. Seafoods fulfill the modern conception of good nutrition. They are high in the protein that contains the important amino acids, high in mineral content, low in fats—and those fats are of the polyunsaturated type."

Shrimp Salad

½ pound cooked shrimp,
peeled and chopped
2 stalks celery, chopped

2 hard boiled eggs, chopped
¼ cup sweet pickles, chopped
5 tablespoons mayonnaise

Add chopped shrimp to the rest of the ingredients, using just enough mayonnaise to hold the mixture together. Chill. Serve on a bed of lettuce. Serves 4.

Cold Shrimp Bisque

¾ pound cooked shrimp
peeled and chopped
1 quart milk

1 tablespoon prepared
mustard
1 tablespoon sugar

1 tablespoon sour pickles,   1 teaspoon salt
  chopped

Combine all the ingredients and chill until ready to serve. This delicious cold soup will serve 4 to 6 persons.

Baked Stuffed Shrimp

1 pound raw shrimp   1 teaspoon Worcestershire sauce
1 pound crabmeat   ½ teaspoon dry mustard
2 slices fresh white bread,   ½ teaspoon salt
  cubed   ¼ cup onion, finely chopped
2 tablespoons mayonnaise   ¼ cup green pepper,
½ teaspoon Tabasco sauce   finely chopped
              ½ cup melted butter

Peel the shells from the uncooked shrimp, leaving the shells at the very tip of the tail in place. Split each shrimp lengthwise down the back and spread them open in butterfly fashion.

Combine crabmeat, bread cubes, mayonnaise, Tabasco sauce, Worcestershire, mustard and salt in a mixing bowl. Saute onion and green pepper in 2 tablespoons butter until tender; then add to the crabmeat mixture. Stuff the centers of each shrimp with the stuffing mixture and squeeze together slightly. Place shrimp, tail end up, on a shallow, greased baking dish and brush each with melted butter. Bake at 400° F. for 10 to 15 minutes, or until browned. Serves 6.

Shrimp with Beans

2 tablespoons butter   ½ cup cooked, mashed
1 pound raw shrimp,   brown beans
  peeled   1 finely chopped onion
1 clove garlic, finely chopped   1 tablespoon cornstarch
              Salt and pepper to taste

Heat butter in large frying pan. Add shrimps and cook for 5 minutes. Blend together beans (mashed), garlic, onion and cornstarch in ½ cup of water and add to shrimps. If the mixture seems too thick and pasty, it may be thinned with more water. Cover frying pan and cook for 5 minutes. Salt and pepper to taste and serve immediately. Serves 4.

Savory Sauce Shrimp

2 tablespoons butter	1 tablespoon Worcestershire
⅓ cup onion,	sauce
finely chopped	1 tablespoon lemon juice
⅓ cup green pepper	⅛ teaspoon curry powder
finely chopped	½ teaspoon salt
2 tablespoons flour	1 dash cayenne pepper
1⅓ cups vegetable juice	1 pound cooked shrimp,
1 pound cooked shrimp,	peeled
peeled	

Melt butter in frying pan and saute the onion and green pepper until tender. Remove pan from heat and slowly stir in flour, blending well. Slowly pour in vegetable juice and stir. Return to heat and cook, stirring constantly until thick and smooth. Add remaining ingredients and simmer very slowly over low flame for 10 minutes.

Pour the sauce over individual servings of boiled whole shrimp that have been prepared while making the sauce. Serves 4.

Live shrimps have a semi-transparent appearance, but upon cooking they turn a pink or reddish color. The tail meat is the only part of the shrimp that is eaten, and this meat is of a firm white texture which is very tender and sweet when properly cooked.

Butter Fried Shrimp

Small raw shrimp, peeled	Salt and pepper
Butter	Dry white wine (optional)

Small shrimp may be fried whole but larger shrimps should be cup into two or more pieces. Sprinkle shrimps with salt and pepper and allow to stand for 15 to 20 minutes. Fry in butter for a few minutes on each side, or until browned. A dash of white wine may be added to the frying pan if you like. You can vary the amounts to serve as many persons as you like. Figure 1 to 1½ cups per serving.

Deep Fried Shrimp

2 cups raw peeled shrimp, small to medium	1 egg
	¼ cup milk
1 cup dry bread crumbs, fine	Salt and pepper to taste

Sprinkle salt and pepper over shrimps and allow to stand for 15 to 20 minutes. Make a batter of whole eggs and milk and dip each shrimp in it; then roll them in bread crumbs. Fry in hot, deep fat until golden brown. Serve with cocktail or tartar sauce.

Tomatoes Stuffed with Shrimp

4 large tomatoes	1 cup shrimp, cooked and
1 cup bread crumbs	peeled
1 tablespoon butter	Salt and pepper to taste

Cut off the tops and remove the pulp from each tomato, leaving only a thin shell. Melt butter, add tomato pulp and cook until thick. Season with salt and pepper. Add 1 cup of finely chopped shrimp and enough bread crumbs to make a mixture of stuffing consistency.

Fill the tomato shells with stuffing, cover with bread crumbs and place a dab of butter on top of each. Bake in a 375° F. oven until lightly browned. Serves 4.

Shrimp Mousse

1 cup shrimp, cooked and peeled	½ cup sweetened pineapple juice
2 tablespoons unflavored gelatin	½ teaspoon salt
	1 tablespoon lime juice
½ cup mayonnaise	1 cup pineapple chunks
⅓ cup cold water	¼ cup celery, chopped

Stir gelatin into the cold water and dissolve over hot water in a double boiler. When completely dissolved, blend in mayonnaise. Stir in pineapple juice, lime juice and salt. Chill mixture until it begins to thicken. When slightly thickened, add celery, shrimp and pineapple chunks. Spoon into individual molds and refrigerate until set. Serves 6.

Curried Shrimp

1 pound shrimp, fresh or frozen	1 pinch of powdered ginger
	½ teaspoon salt
3 tablespoons butter	½ cup chicken bouillon
⅓ cup chopped onion	1 cup milk
3 tablespoons flour	1 dash concentrated
1 teaspoon curry powder	lemon juice

Boil and peel shrimp in the regular manner. Melt butter in a sauce pan and cook the onion until tender. Stir in flour, curry powder, ginger and salt, blending well. Next, slowly add the chicken bouillon and milk. Simmer slowly over low heat until thickened, stirring constantly. Add shrimp and lemon juice and cook until just heated through. Serves 4.

Sweet and Sour Shrimp

1 pound raw shrimp	¼ cup white vinegar
1/3 cup brown sugar	1 cup canned pineapple chunks
1½ tablespoons soy sauce	(and juice from the can)
2 tablespoons cornstarch	½ teaspoon salt

Boil and peel shrimp in the regular manner. In a saucepan mix brown sugar, soy sauce, juice from the canned pineapple, cornstarch, salt, and vinegar. Cook over low heat until thickened, stirring constantly. Add pineapple chunks and cook an additional 3 or 4 minutes and remove from heat. Add shrimp and allow to stand for 15 to 20 minutes. Bring the entire mixture to the boiling point just prior to serving. Serves 4.

Shrimp for a Crowd
(Shrimp and Cheese Casserole)

3 cups white rice, cooked	1 onion, chopped

1½ pounds grated
   Cheddar cheese
3 eggs
¾ cup vegetable oil

4 cups shrimp, cooked and
   peeled
1½ cans (13 ounces each)
   evaporated milk

Salt and pepper to taste

Mix together all ingredients. Bake in a large casserole dish at 350° F. for 45 minutes. Serves 15.

Chinese Shrimp

1 cup celery, chopped
½ cup onion, chopped
3 tablespoons pimento
1 can (4 ounces)
   mushrooms, drained
1 tablespoon butter
¼ cup water

¼ cup chopped nuts
   (Cashews best)
½ pound cooked shrimp,
   peeled
1 cup Medium-thick White
   Sauce (See Chapter Nine)
2 (3 ounces each)
   Chinese noodles

Combine celery, onion and water in a saucepan with salted water and cook until soft. Drain off water. Combine cooked celery and onion with mushrooms, nuts, pimentos and shrimp. Mix in white sauce and blend well. Layer the bottom of a greased baking dish with half of the noodles, cover with the shrimp mixture and top with the remaining noodles. Bake in a 350° F. oven for 30 minutes and serve hot. Serves 4.

Shrimp Boats

1 pound small raw shrimp
¼ cup white wine vinegar
¼ cup vegetable oil
½ cup dry sherry

1 tablespoon salt
1 small onion, finely chopped
1 tablespoon sugar
4 avocados (optional)

Peel and clean the raw shimp—if large, cut into small pieces. Combine in a saucepan the shrimp, vinegar, oil, sherry, salt, sugar, and onion and allow to simmer gently for about 5 or 6 minutes. Then cool.

Peel avocados and cut into halves. Use the shrimp with just a tiny bit of the sauce as a filling for the avocado centers. If served without the avocados, these shrimp are simply delicious served on toothpicks with the sauce in a separate bowl. Serves 3 to 4.

Shrimp and Tomato Aspic

2 tablespoons unflavored gelatin	1 dash salt
1 cup tomato juice	½ cup cucumber, chopped
1 teaspoon lemon juice	½ teaspoon oregano
	½ teaspoon tarragon

1 cup cooked shrimp, peeled

Soak gelatin in ¼ cup of tomato juice to soften. Heat remaining tomato juice and add to the gelatin mixture, stirring constantly until dissolved. Add lemon juice and a dash of salt. Place in refrigerator and cool until mixture begins to set, then mix in the cucumber, oregano, tarragon and shrimp. Spoon into individual molds and chill until set. This dish goes well with a topping of cottage cheese seasoned with salt and pepper. Serves 2.

Shrimp Chowder

4 slices, uncooked bacon, cut in small pieces	1 pound cooked shrimp, peeled
1 onion, chopped	1 cup boiling water
2 small raw potatoes, diced	2 cups light cream (or milk)
	2 tablespoons butter

Salt and pepper to taste

Fry onion and bacon together until browned. Add potato and boiling water. Cover and cook until potatoes are tender. Lower heat to the simmering point and add shrimp, cream, butter and salt and pepper, stirring constantly until heated through. Makes a delicious hot chowder. Serves 6.

Shrimp Omelet

½ cup small cooked shrimp, peeled	3 eggs
	Salt and pepper to taste

Butter

Blend together all ingredients except the butter. Fry in butter over medium heat until firm. Lift up the side of the omelet occasionally to allow loose mixture to flow to the underside. Do not stir.

All shellfish meats are quite delicious when made into omelets, and there are hundreds of variations that you can concoct. Fold onto heated platters and serve with toast for a really good breakfast dish. Serves 2.

Shrimp Pie

2 cups cooked shrimp,
  peeled and chopped
4 tablespoons mayonnaise
2 tablespoons grated cheese
  (any variety)

2 tablespoons onion,
  finely chopped
1 dash lemon juice
Pie crust dough (enough to
  make top and bottom crusts
  for a 9-inch pie)

Mix all ingredients except pie dough together in a bowl. Roll out pie dough. Line 9-inch pie pan with dough. Fill with shrimp mixture. Cover pie with dough to form a top crust. Bake in a 375° F. oven until crust turns golden brown. Serves 4.

Shrimp Marinara

1 onion, chopped
¼ cup butter
½ teaspoon garlic salt
1½ cups canned stewed
  tomatoes, drained

1 teaspoon oregano
2 bay leaves
1 pound raw shrimp, peeled
Cooked rice

Saute onion in butter and garlic salt until tender. Add tomatoes, bay leaves and oregano and simmer for 15 minutes. Add shrimp and simmer an additional 5 to 10 minutes or until shrimp is pink and tender. Serve over the top of a bed of cooked rice. Garnish with parsley and grated cheese if you like it fancy. Serves 4.

Shrimp New Orleans

6 tablespoons butter

1 pinch garlic salt

3 tomatoes, diced
1 onion, chopped
3 stalks celery, chopped
½ teaspoon thyme

Salt and pepper to taste
1 pound raw shrimp,
   peeled, and diced
Buttered toast

Melt butter in a saucepan and add tomatoes, celery, onion, thyme, garlic salt and salt and pepper to taste. Bring to the boiling point then lower heat, cover, and simmer gently for 20 minutes.

After 20 minutes add shrimp to the cooking vegetables and continue to simmer for another 10 minutes, or until shrimp becomes tender. Serve hot over buttered toast. Serves 4.

Plain Shrimp Aspic

1 pound cooked shrimp,
   peeled
2 tablespoons unflavored
   gelatin

¾ cup cold water
1½ cups chicken bouillon
½ cup catsup
2 teaspoons lemon juice

2 tablespoons green olives, chopped

Dissolve gelatin in cold water; then add hot chicken bouillon and lemon juice, stirring constantly until the gelatin has completely dissolved. Set aside and allow to partially set.

Add catsup, olives and shrimp after mixture has begun to jell. Spoon into individual molds and place into the refrigerator to chill and set Serves 6.

Shrimp Pie

¾ pound cooked, peeled, and
   cleaned shrimp, fresh or
   frozen
      or
3 cans (4½ ounces each) shrimp
1 cup onion rings
2 tablespoons melted fat or oil
1 can (10½ ounces) condensed
   cream of celery soup

1 can (4 ounces) mushrooms,
   stems and pieces, drained
1 teaspoon Worcestershire
   sauce
Dash pepper
2 cups seasoned mashed
   potatoes
1 tablespoon chopped parsley
Paprika

Thaw frozen shrimp or drain canned shrimp. Rinse canned shrimp with cold water. Cook onions in fat until tender. Combine all ingredients except potatoes, parsley, and paprika. Combine potatoes and parsley. Pour shrimp mixture into a well-greased pie pan, 10 x 1½ inches. Top with a border of potatoes. Sprinkle with paprika. Bake in a very hot oven, 450° F., for 15 to 20 minutes or until lightly browned. Serves 6.

Chapter Seven

Crabs

ABOUT CRABS

CRAB, THE COMMON name popularly applied to various arthropodous animals, most of which belong to the short-tailed (Brachyera) division of decapod Crustaceans. There are over one thousand known varieties of true crab, most of which have no common names.

The body of a crab is usually short and compressed, the abdomen is short, there are one to four reduced abdominal appendages, seldom any tail paddles, and short antennae. The two great forward claws are generally larger in the male than in the female.

Crabs vary greatly in size and color, as might be expected from the wide distribution and great number of the species. The Giant Crab of Japan (Macrocheria kaempferi), although only a foot wide across the main shell and 18 inches lengthwise, has such a long set of legs it is occasionally able to extend itself 15 feet in width from tip to tip. At the opposite extreme, are many species that only measure a fraction of an inch across. There are even species which are so small that only by use of a powerful microscope can their physical make-up be distinguished.

Crabs feed chiefly upon other animals and animal matter, being in the main classed as scavengers. There are many land crabs which are mainly vegetarians and do great damage to crops in certain parts of the world. All crabs, except land crabs, carry their eggs until they are hatched.

The majority of crabs are of the marine variety and frequent shallow waters. Some land crabs migrate in companies to the sea for egg-laying purposes. There is also a curious fellow called the pea crab which lives inside bivalves, chiefly the oyster.

Like other Crustaceans, crabs must periodically shed their shells. This operation is most frequent in young crabs at their period of most rapid growth. In most cases, crabs are able to regenerate an amputated limb, although several molts of its shell may be required to grow back a full-sized limb.

By the study of fossils, crabs are known to date from at least the Mesozic age. Fossil crabs first appear in the Jurassic age, but these fossils are of the family Dromiacea, much smaller than the modern species.

THE COMMON EDIBLE CRABS

The crab is a familiar and favorite shellfish all over America, and the following are some of the most commonly eaten varieties and where they are found.

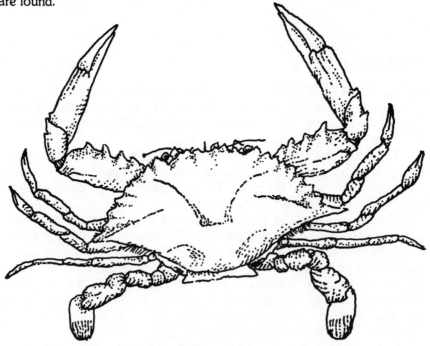

BLUE CRAB

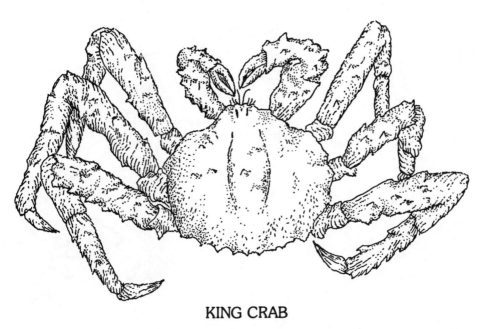

KING CRAB

Among the best known edible crabs of America are: the king crabs and tanner crabs found in the North Pacific off Alaska; the big Dungeness crabs found all the way from Alaska southwards to Baja California; red crabs and rock crabs found on the Pacific coast; rock crabs and Jonah crabs found in the New England states, as well as in California, being close relatives of the Dungeness crabs; stone crabs found from North Carolina to the Gulf Coast of Texas; green crabs found from Maine to New Jersey; lady crabs (sometimes called calico crabs or sand crabs) found from Cape Cod to Florida; and the popular blue crabs or hard crabs found along the Atlantic and Gulf coasts.

All crabs which are large enough to provide a decent amount of meat are edible. However, most have been entirely neglected as a source of food for one reason or another. Usually some sort of false prejudice is to blame.

The soft-shelled crabs of the fish markets are swimming crabs. Like all crabs, these swimmers periodically cast off their old shells, and when caught before their new shell hardens, they form the soft-shelled crabs for our tables. Thus you see it is not a species of crab, but rather the condition of a crab, that constitutes a soft-shelled crab. Soft-shells are considered a great delicacy for which people commonly pay a premium price. In the recipe section on crabs, I will discuss these soft-shelled crabs in further detail.

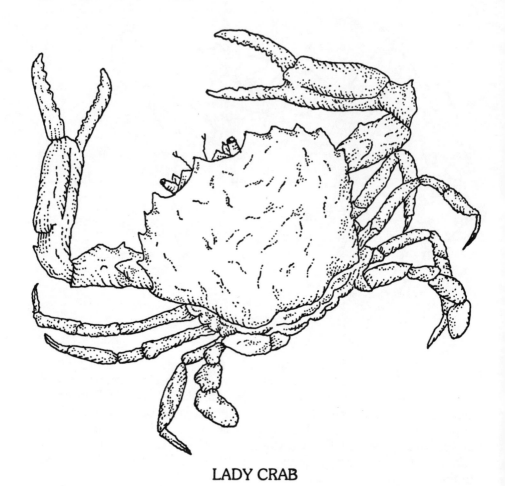

LADY CRAB

BUYING CRABS

If you can afford the price of live crabs from your local fish market, be sure that there are signs of movement in their legs before you purchase them. Live crabs can stand some limited storage in your refrigerator, but should not be stored for longer than 24 hours. Dead shellfish, as a rule, should never be used for food, even though lobsters and crabs may be safe enough if they smell all right and their flesh remains firm. I would not fool with dead crabs unless I was certain that they had died while in my refrigerator within a half hour or so. Even then it's doubtful that I would use them.

Crab meat can also be purchased in cans and in the frozen state from your local supermarket. Crabmeat purchased in these ways can be used equally well in any recipe calling for crabmeat.

CATCHING CRABS

Crabs may be easily caught in shallow water with dip nets, or in some cases, by simply poking them with the end of a long pole, which, in their aggressiveness, they will sieze with their strong claws long enough to allow you to gently pull them to the surface and scoop up with a dip net.

Crabs which dwell in moderate depths are taken in crab-pots (similar to lobster pots) baited with almost any kind of scrap fish or meat. Another method, used in deeper water, and off the sides of wharves, etc., is by use of hoop-nets, which are coarse meshed, shallow nets, resembling a large deep dish in shape. These nets are baited in the center and lowered to the bottom so as to lie in a flat position. When there is reason to suppose that a crab might be on the net eating the bait, the net is pulled swiftly and steadily to the surface before the crab has a chance to escape.

On the Atlantic coast, the blue crab is caught on hand-lines baited with meat, fish, or chicken necks. A piece of this bait is simply tied onto the end of a string and lowered into the water. When a crab begins to nibble on the bait he may be gently pulled to the surface and dipped up with a net. (Crabs are stupid and will keep eating your bait as you pull them to the surface.)

It is very easy to catch your own supply of crabs in almost any part of the U.S. bordering on the seasore, or even in estuaries which lead directly to the salt water.

Having at one time been a professional crab fisherman, I can attest to the ease with which anyone, with even a rudimentary knowledge of catching crabs, can get himself a mess for the table in no time flat. Crabbing is indeed the proverbial "child's-play."

HOW TO CLEAN SOFT-SHELLED CRABS

Remember that crabs must be alive when purchased from your seafood market. You may have the fish man clean your soft-shelled crabs, or do it yourself at home.

Wash the crabs carefully in cold water, removing all dirt, sand, and slime. Do not run hot water over them as this treatment will tend to destroy their flavor. With a sharp knife, cut off the apron that folds under the body from the rear. Cut off face of the crab at the point behind the eyes. Remove the spongy, feathery like material under the side points of the shell by gently lifting the points and scraping out this material. Again, rinse the crabs under cold water, then dry on soft absorbent towels.

When cooked, the entire soft-shelled crab which has been cleaned by the above method is wholly edible.

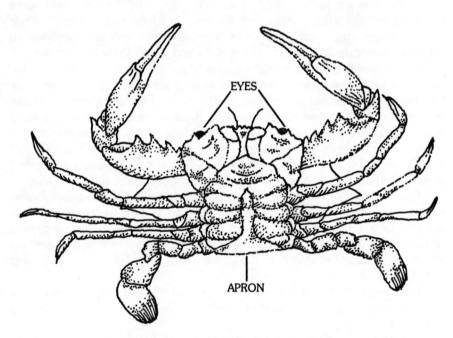

THE UNDERSIDE OF A CRAB SHOWING APRON AREA, ETC.

CLEANING COOKED CRABS

Wash live crabs to remove all dirt and slime. Plunge, head first, into a pot of rapidly boiling, salted water (3 tablespoons salt to 1 quart water). Never cook more than 4 crabs at a time. Cover the pot and cook crabs at a rolling boil for 15 minutes. Lift out with tongs and cool as rapidly as possible until they reach the point where you can handle them. Now force the upper and lower shell halves apart. Turn the crab so that the "apron" side is up (the apron is on the crab's underside and has a design like an apron—see illustration). Remove the "apron" from the body of the crab with a sharp knife, and discard the spongy matter located on each side under the top shell ("devil's fingers," or gills) and the lungs located underneath the eyes. Hold the crab under cold running water to wash out the green and brown fatty material. Crack the claws with a nutcracker or light hammer and chill in the refrigerator.

Your crab is now cooked and cleaned and is ready for eating on the spot by simply picking out the meat and dipping it into a sauce, or for use in preparing your favorite crabmeat recipe. There is delicious red and white crab meat located in both the front claws, as well as in the body cavity.

CRAB RECIPES

Maryland Crab

2 tablespoons butter
1 tablespoon flour
2 quarts milk
¼ cup diced onion
2 cups crab meat

2 tablespoons parsley, chopped
½ cup celery, pre-cooked
1 teaspoon salt
1 dash pepper
Whipped cream

Melt butter in a saucepan and add the flour, blending well. Next add the 2 quarts of milk and bring to the boiling point. Add onion, parsley, celery, salt and pepper and cook mixture until slightly thickened. Add crab meat and allow it to cook until heated through, but do not boil. Serve hot topped with whipped cream. Serves 6 to 8.

Crab and Tomato Bisque

1 cup crab meat
2 cups milk
1 cup tomato juice

2 tablespoons butter
2 tablespoons flour
½ teaspoon salt

1 pinch pepper

Melt butter in the top of a double boiler, add flour and blend in thoroughly. Add milk gradually and cook until thickened. Add seasonings and crab meat. Just before serving, heat the tomato juice in a separate pan. When it is hot, add the tomato juice gradually to the first mixture, and blend in well. Serve hot as soon as removed from the stove. Serves 4.

Crab Louis

2 cups crab meat
¾ cup mayonnaise
¼ cup catsup
2 tablespoons parsley, chopped

2 teaspoons vinegar
½ teaspoon Worcestershire
  sauce
½ teaspoon horseradish

Blend together the mayonnaise, sauces, and spices. Mix gently into the crab meat. Chill thoroughly and serve on a bed of lettuce. Serves 4.

Cracked Crabs

Boil crabs and pick out their meat. Set in refrigerator to chill thoroughly.

Prepare a dressing of ¾ cup olive oil, ¼ cup fresh lime juice, ¼ teaspoon salt, and a dash of tabasco sauce. Place some dressing in individual bowls for dipping. The boiled crabmeat is eaten after dipping it into the sauce. If you serve whole crabs and allow each person to pick out their own meat, it will be found a messy dish indeed, in fact almost as messy as it is delicious. For a beverage to go with cracked crab, nothing beats ice cold beer. Allow about three medium-sized crabs per person.

Crab Meat au Gratin

2 cups crab meat
1 cup Medium-thick White
  Sauce (See Chapter Nine)
¼ teaspoon salt
¼ teaspoon paprika

2 tablespoons buttered
  bread crumbs
2 tablespoons grated
  Parmesan cheese

Add crab meat to white sauce and seasonings, and place in individual baking dishes. Sprinkle bread crumbs mixed with grated cheese over the top and bake at 350° F. for 15 minutes. Serve hot with a garnish of parsley and lemon wedges. Serves 4.

If you sit and watch a bunch of crabs walk about for awhile, you will always come away quite amused. They move about in a comical, queer sort of sideways motion instead of backwards and forwards. Crabs found on the shore are rather slow moving as a rule, while the swimming crabs are considerably more active and agile.

Crab Meat Newburg

4 tablespoons butter
2 cups crab meat
¼ teaspoon salt
1 dash pepper
5 tablespoons dry sherry

¼ cup mushrooms, fresh or
  canned
1 cup cream, light
3 egg yolks
4 slices buttered toast

Melt butter in the top of a double boiler over hot water. Add crab meat and sprinkle with salt and pepper. Add the sherry and mushrooms, and allow to cook for about 2 minutes, stirring constantly. Add cream and allow mixture to heat up until it begins to steam. Beat egg yolks lightly and stir into the mixture two or three minutes before serving. During this last operation, keep stirring frequently over hot, but not boiling water. Serves 4.

This recipe is also delicious with lobster or shrimp substituted for the crab meat.

Baked Soft-Shell Crab

1 dozen soft-shell crabs	Salt and pepper to taste
¼ cup melted butter	1 cup fine bread crumbs

Clean crabs as outlined in the directions above, wash under cold water and dry as much as possible.

Dip each crab in melted butter and sprinkle with salt and pepper; then roll each crab in bread crumbs. Place in a shallow baking pan and cook in at 400° F. for 5 minutes, or until browned. Serve with tartar sauce. Serves 4 to 6 depending on size of crabs.

Buttered Crab Meat

¼ cup butter	1 cup cooked crab meat
	Salt and pepper to taste

Melt butter in a frying pan (make sure butter is quite hot, but do not burn it). Add crab meat and cook under low heat for 5 to 6 minutes (do not brown). Season to taste with salt and pepper and serve as hot as humanly possible. Serves 2.

Among the foods for which aphrodisiac powers have been ascribed are crayfish tails, crabs, caviar, and sharks fin soup—the last being one of the classic Chinese love potions.

"Snug Harbor" Crab Meat Feast

This recipe originally came from the Tea Room of L. S. Ayres and Co. whose manager, Miss Veronica Morrissey, used to make a practice of swapping recipes with the customers, to the mutual benefit of both parties.

½ cup medium-thick
  white sauce
2½ teaspoons onion juice
1½ teaspoons Worcestershire
  sauce

½ cup fresh bread, cubed
½ cup mayonnaise
2 teaspoons lemon juice
Salt and pepper to taste
1¼ pounds fresh crab meat

2 tablespoons browned butter

Blend white sauce (recipe in sauce section of this book), onion juice, Worcestershire sauce and bread cubes. When this mixture is cool, fold in mayonnaise, lemon juice, salt and pepper. Gently toss crab meat with the browned butter, then add to the white sauce mixture and fold in gently. Place in baking dishes and brown at 450° F. for 10 to 15 minutes. Serve immediately. Serves 8.

Toasted Crab Sandwiches

¾ cup crab meat,
  pre-cooked
2 teaspoons horseradish
½ teaspoon Worcestershire
  sauce
1 dash Tabasco sauce

1 teaspoon lemon juice
2 tablespoons mayonnaise
  Salt and pepper (optional)
6 slices bread
6 thin slices of
  Cheddar cheese

Mix together crab meat, horseradish, Worcestershire and Tabasco sauces, and lemon juice. Add mayonnaise to moisten. If desired, add salt and pepper to taste. Toast the bread slices on one side. Spread the untoasted side of the bread with crab mixture and top with a cheese slice. Place under broiler until the cheese browns. Serve hot. Serves 6.

Crab Meat Stew

1 small onion, sliced
2 tablespoons butter

2 cups crab meat, diced
3 cups milk

Salt and pepper to taste

Cook a few slices of onion in the butter, then add crab meat, milk, and salt and pepper to taste. Heat and serve. That's all there is to the preparations of a delicious crab meat stew which will serve 3 to 4 persons.

Crab Cocktail

¼ cup mayonnaise	Juice of 2 limes
2 cups crab meat	1 dash pepper

Salt and pepper to taste

Combine mayonnaise with crab meat. Add lime juice, a generous dash of pepper, and salt to taste. Chill the mixture thoroughly. Serve in chilled cocktail glasses on a bed of lettuce. Serves 6.

Crab Meat Sauterne

2 cups Medium-thick White Sauce (See Chapter Nine)	Pinch garlic salt
1 cup crab meat	¾ cup Sauterne wine
¾ cup butter	1¾ cups dry bread crumbs
	Grated American cheese

Add crab meat to white sauce. Divide the crab meat and sauce mixture into 6 1-cup individual greased baking dishes. Prepare a topping by creaming the butter, adding garlic salt and wine to it and gradually the topping among the 6 baking dishes, then sprinkle the tops with grated cheese. Bake at 375° F. for 30 minutes, or until browned lightly on top. Serves 6.

When at the seashore, you may have to keep a sharp eye out for some types of crabs. Some are experts at disguising themselves, and many types employ a covering of seaweed in order to hide from their enemies. Others make a practice of burrowing just beneath the sand for the purposes of hiding as well as lying in wait for passing prey. It seems that the disguise business works both ways—to hide from enemies, or to lie in wait for prey.

Crab and Chicken Delight

6 tablespoons butter	3 cups chicken, cooked and chopped
6 tablespoons flour	2 cups crab meat, cooked
1 teaspoon salt	2 cups green peas, cooked
1 garlic clove, minced	8 slices bacon, crisp and crumbled
Pepper to taste	
1½ cups chicken bouillon	

2 cups sour cream

1 can cream of mushroom
soup, concentrated

Make a white sauce from melted butter, flour and salt and pepper. Add chicken bouillon and sour cream to sauce, and stir until well blended. Add chicken and crab meat. Simmer for 20 minutes, stirring often. When ready to serve, add cooked peas, crumbled bacon bits, sauce, garlic, and mushroom soup. Heat mixture and serve on a bed of cooked rice. Serves 6.

Crab Meat Imperial

2 cups crab meat, cooked

1 cup celery, finely chopped

½ cup green pepper,
    finely chopped

3 teaspoons onion, grated

3 tablespoons French dressing

1 clove garlic, chopped

1 cup mayonnaise

½ teaspoon curry powder

Mix together all ingredients except curry powder and mayonnaise and allow to stand until ready to serve. Add curry powder to mayonnaise and toss into mixture. Serve chilled on a bed of lettuce. Parsley and boiled egg slices may be used as a garnish. Serves 2.

Stuffed Crabs

2 tablespoons onion, grated

4 tablespoons butter

2 cups crab meat

¾ cups bread crumbs, dry

¼ cup water

1 tablespoon lemon juice

1 teaspoon parsley, dry

2 hard boiled eggs, grated

Sauté onion in butter until soft; add crab meat, bread crumbs, water and lemon juice. Cook 10 to 15 minutes. Add parsley and eggs to mixture and place in crab shells or individual baking dishes; sprinkle tops with bread crumbs. Heat in oven and serve. Serves 4 to 6.

Crab Meat and Broccoli

1 package (13 ounces) frozen
    broccoli spears (thawed)

1 teaspoon mustard, prepared

1 teaspoon onion, grated

1 cup crab meat, cooked   1 teaspoon grated Parmesan
¼ cup mayonnaise   cheese
                2 tablespoons lemon juice

Combine all ingredients in a baking dish and bake for 20 minutes in a 350° F. oven. Serves 4.

Crab Meat and Asparagus

1 cup crab meat   ¼ teaspoon salt
1 can (14 ounces)   1 cup White Sauce
   asparagus tips   (See Chapter Nine)
1 (4 ounces) can   1 cup grated Parmesan
   mushrooms, drained   cheese

Arrange layers of crab meat, asparagus tips, mushrooms, and salt in a well greased (or buttered) two quart baking dish. Cover with white sauce and top with grated cheese. Bake at 350° F. for 30 minutes. Serves 4.

Breakfast Crab

Melt some butter in a frying pan, brown small bits of crab meat in it, then add lightly beaten eggs and proceed as you would for scrambled eggs. This makes a different and delicious breakfast dish.

Jiffy-Canny Crab Meat Soup

1 can condensed pea soup   2 cans water
1 can condensed bouillon   1½ cups cooked crab meat
   (chicken or beef)   1 dash dry sherry

Mix together all the ingredients except the sherry; heat to the boiling point. Add the sherry and serve hot. Serves 4 to 6.

Hawaiian Crab Meat

2 cups crab meat, cooked   ¼ cup mayonnaise
½ cup chopped celery   ¼ cup catsup

½ cup chopped watercress   1 teaspoon lemon juice
    1 can (11 ounces) sliced pineapple, drained

Combine crab meat with celery and watercress. Combine mayonnaise, catsup, and lemon juice and mix lightly into the crab mixture. Place in mounds atop pineapple slices and serve cold on a bed of lettuce. Serves 4.

Crab and Cheese Casserole

2 cups crab meat   ¾ cup celery, chopped
8 slices bread, buttered   4 eggs, lightly beaten
  and cubed   Salt and pepper to taste
2½ cups milk   1 can cream of mushroom
1 small onion, grated   soup, concentrated
1 green pepper, chopped   Grated Parmesan cheese

Combine all ingredients except Mushroom soup and Parmesan cheese. Allow to stand for 30 minutes, then bake in a 375° F. oven for 25 minutes. Add Mushroom soup and a generous sprinkling of cheese. Bake for another 15 minutes. Serve piping hot. Serves 4 to 6.

Creamed Crab au Gratin

4 cups Medium-thick White   1 cup cooked mushrooms
  Sauce (See Chapter Nine)   ½ cup green pepper, chopped
1 cup cheddar cheese, grated   2 tablespoons pimentos
1 pound cooked crab meat   1 cup bread crumbs
              Butter

Add cheese to white sauce and heat until mixture is smooth and cheese is melted. Add crab meat and bring mixture just to the boiling point (but do not boil). Add mushrooms, green pepper and pimento. Fill individual 2-cup baking dishes with mixture and cover with a thin layer of bread crumbs and a dab of butter. Bake at 350° F. for about 20 minutes, or until top is light brown. Serves 6.

Crab Meat Treats

1 cup crab meat, cooked   1 teaspoon lemon juice

3 packages cream cheese
  (3 oz. size)
1 dash Worcestershire sauce

3 tomatoes, sliced
10 Cheddar cheese slices
8 toast squares

Mix crab meat, cream cheese, Worcestershire sauce and lemon juice together, blending well. Spread on toast squares and top with a slice of tomato and a slice of cheddar cheese. Place under broiler until cheese melts and begins to bubble. Serve hot. Serves 4.

Crab Meat on Toast

2 cups crab meat, cooked
½ can concentrated
  cream of mushroom soup

1 tablespoon white wine
Buttered toast

Simmer crab meat with thick mushroom soup and wine until heated through. Stir often. Serve on buttered toast on hot platters. Serves 2.

Quick Crab Bisque

1 can concentrated tomato soup
1 can concentrated pea soup

1¼ cups milk
2 cups cooked crab meat

Combine all ingredients with enough water to bring mixture to a soupy consistency. Season to taste and serve hot. Serves 4.

Lobster or shrimp could be used equally as well in this recipe.

Crabcakes

1 cup crab meat, cooked
3 eggs, well beaten
3 tablespoons green pepper,
  chopped

1 teaspoon onion, grated
1 dash salt
1 dash pepper

Combine all ingredients and mix well. Drop by spoonsful onto a hot greased griddle and cook until brown and puffy. Serves 2.

These cakes are really pancakes of a sort, and go really well with a topping of ginger sauce or hot lemon sauce (see Chapter Nine for these recipes).

Crab Meat Buns

3 hamburger buns, halved
½ pound crab meat, cooked
1 3-ounce package
   cream cheese
1 dash Worcestershire sauce

1 tablespoon catsup
1 tablespoon mayonnaise
1 tomato (6 slices)
   Grated Cheddar cheese
Salt and pepper to taste

Butter buns and place a slice of tomato on each. Season with salt and pepper. Mix together crab meat, Worcestershire sauce, mayonnaise, cream cheese and catsup. Place mixture over tomato slices on buns and sprinkle with grated cheese. Bake in a 375° F. oven until bun is sufficiently toasted and cheese is melted. Serves 3 to 6.

Crab Sauce with Spaghetti

1 pound crab meat; fresh,
   frozen, or pasteurized
     or
3 cans (6½ or 7½ ounces each)
   crab meat
½ cup chopped onion
  ½ cup chopped celery
  2 cloves garlic,
   finely chopped
  2 tablespoons chopped
   parsley

¼ cup butter or margarine,
   melted
1 cup canned tomatoes
1 can (8 ounces) tomato
   sauce
¼ teaspoon salt
½ teaspoon paprika
   Dash pepper
3 cups cooked spaghetti
   Grated Parmesan cheese

Thaw frozen crab meat. Drain crab meat. Remove any remaining shell or cartilage. Cut crab meat into ½-inch pieces. Cook onion, celery, garlic, and parsley in butter until tender. Add tomatoes, tomato sauce, and seasonings. Simmer for 20 minutes, stirring occasionally. Add crab meat; heat. Serve over spaghetti. Garnish with cheese sprinkled over the top. Serves 6.

Chapter Eight

Mixed Shellfish Recipes

Lobster and Scallops in Curry

This makes a grand dish to serve during the fall when both lobsters and scallops are in season.

½ cup lobster meat 1 teaspoon curry powder
½ cup scallop meat 1 teaspoon tomato paste
4 tablespoons onion, chopped ½ cup light cream

Cut pre-cooked lobster meat to the size of scallops and cook both together in a frying pan with butter. Add finely chopped onion and continue to fry until onions begin to sizzle. Stir in the curry powder, cover fry pan, and cook for 3 minutes. Add the tomato paste and thin the entire mixture with cream. Simmer for 10 minutes, season to taste, and serve hot. Serves 2.

Shellfish Lovers' Delight

2 eggs 3 tablespoons flour
½ cup crab meat 2 cups milk

½ cup lobster meat	½ teaspoon salt
½ cup clams, finely chopped	½ cup mushrooms, sliced
2 tablespoons butter	4 tablespoons white wine, dry

Melt the butter in a saucepan and stir in the flour. Add 1½ cups of the milk slowly, and stir until mixture thickens. Add chopped shellfish to the sauce, then beat the eggs together with the remaining ½ cup of milk and add to the sauce first prepared, stirring in well. Place heated ingredients into a well greased, 1 quart casserole dish and bake at 350° F. for 25 or 30 minutes. If you like, you can top this casserole with bread crumbs or grated cheese. Serves 4.

New England Clambake (for a crowd)

Clambakes are a New England tradition that are both fun to participate in, and a feast that is not soon forgotten.

To begin with, dig a pit in the sand high enough up above the high tide

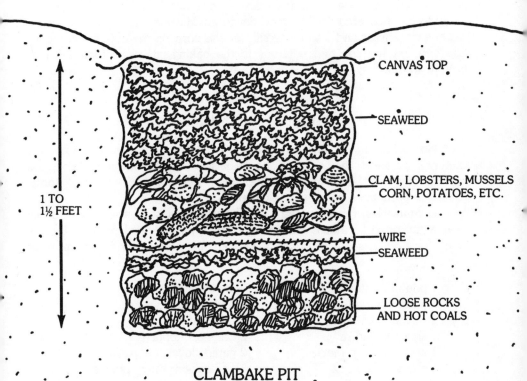

CLAMBAKE PIT

line so that it does not fill with water. Layer the bottom of the pit with large stones. Build a roaring wood fire in the pit and allow it to burn down to a bed of coals with some of the rocks in the bottom showing through the embers.

While waiting for the fire to burn down to a bed of hot coals, prepare the food for baking. For a clambake you will, of course need some clams. Wash a batch of freshly dug clams thoroughly in clean seawater. Plan on at least a quart pail of clams for each person as appetites run high at clambakes. Kill freshly caught, or freshly bought lobsters by piercing their spinal cords with a sharp knife between the body and tail. You might also add some mussels to your meal, if any are available. Corn on the cob and baked potatoes make good additions to a clambake and will roast up nicely in your pit. Wrap these items in foil, but do not wrap the shellfish.

Brush off the ashes from the top of the rocks in the pit, and spread a thin layer of seaweed over the stones. It will help a great deal if you place a piece of coarse wire screening over the top of the seaweed. Now place the lobsters, clams, corn, potatoes, fish, or other ingredients you have selected on top of the seaweed. Cover the pile of food with another generous layer of seaweed. Place a piece of canvas over the top of the final layer of seaweed to keep the steam from escaping. In about 1 hour, the pit will be ready to be uncovered and the food devoured. Have plenty of melted butter ready for the feast and also some salt for the corn on the cob. Note: if you add corn on the cob and potatoes to the baking pit, place them on the bottom so that they will get the most heat.

Flipper's Bouillabaisse

No collection of shellfish recipes would be complete without the author's personal recipe for a bouillabaisse. The following is mine, the virtues of which I shall not expound upon. Perhaps you will try it sometime and pronounce your own judgment.

In Marseilles, France, where Bouillabaisse was born, they seem to use a quantity of garlic that is staggering to the imagination. I prefer a bit less than the French seem to like, but you can suit yourself by adding more or less.

1 pound lobster meat, cooked	½ cup white wine
1 pound crab meat, cooked	2 tablespoons butter
1 pound clam meat, shucked and raw	2 tablespoons flour
	2 onions, chopped
1 pound scallop meat, shucked and raw	2 garlic cloves, chopped
	1½ teaspoons curry powder
½ pound mushrooms, sliced	2 bay leaves

2 cups tomato pulp	1 teaspoon salt

1 dash Tabasco sauce

Melt the butter in a large frying pan and saute the onions, garlic, and flour until they turn golden brown. Transfer these to a large saucepan or kettle and add tomato pulp, 2 cups water, bay leaves, curry powder, tabasco sauce and half of the wine. Simmer for 30 minutes, then add the salt.

Simmer the still raw clams and scallops for 15 minutes in 1½ quarts of water and the remaining ¼ cup of wine. Then add lobster meat, crab meat, mushrooms, and the sauce that was first prepared. Simmer entire mixture for 5 minutes then serve hot. Serves about 12. This will even taste better when reheated as leftovers on the second day.

Cape Sable Supper

2 cups celery, chopped	1 cup lobster
1 green pepper, chopped	1 small can mushrooms
1 cup crab meat	1 cup White Sauce
	(See Chapter Nine)

Cook celery and green pepper in a small amount of water until tender. Combine with other ingredients and blend into 1 cup of white sauce (see sauce chapter for the preparation of the white sauce). Reheat the entire mixture and serve on toast or over a bed of rice. Serves 4.

Curried Shellfish

1 pound assorted shellfish	½ teaspoon curry powder
2½ cups water	1 egg, well beaten
1 teaspoon salt	¼ cup cracker crumbs
4 tablespoons butter	¾ cup boiling water
1 small onion, finely chopped	1 dash lemon juice

Cook the shellfish in 2½ cups water until tender. Chop the meat as finely as possible and set aside for the moment.

Melt a bit of the butter in a frying pan and brown the onion. Add curry powder and continue to cook for another 2 minutes. Add this mixture along with the salt to the shellfish. Form into balls, dip into beaten egg, and roll in cracker crumbs. Melt remaining butter in a large frying pan and fry the balls of shellfish in it until golden brown. Add boiling water and a dash of lemon juice, cover and simmer gently for 20 minutes. Serves 4.

Shellfish Salads

It's easy to prepare simple and delicious shellfish salads by simply mixing cooked, fresh, frozen, or canned shellfish (such as lobster, crab meat, shrimp, etc.) with mayonnaise and seasonings to taste. Serve on a bed of lettuce and garnish with parsley, hard-boiled eggs and/or tomatoes.

Seafood Omelet

5 tablespoons pre-cooked lobster, scallop, crab meat, clam or other seafood	1 dash oregano 1 dash parsley ½ teaspoon salt
1 tablespoon butter	Pepper to taste

Heat the seafood (a combination if you like) and seasonings in butter in a frying pan for 2 minutes. Add beaten eggs and proceed with making an omelet in the ordinary way. Serves 1.

Stuffed Eggs

8 hard-boiled eggs cut in half lengthwise	½ cup mayonnaise ½ teaspoon paprika
1 cup shellfish meat, chopped and drained	Salt and pepper to taste

Remove the yolks from the egg halves and grind them up by rubbing through a coarse strainer. Set them aside for the moment. Fill the egg whites with shellfish meat mixed with mayonnaise, paprika, and seasonings. Spread the ground egg yolks over the tops of the stuffed eggs and serve. Serves 2 to 4.

Molded Shellfish Salad

1 can concentrated Cream of Mushroom soup	1 cup mayonnaise 1 cup celery, chopped
¾ cup cold water	1 cup crabmeat, cooked

2 tablespoons unflavored
  gelatin
3 3-ounce package
  cream cheese

1 cup lobster (or shrimp),
  cooked
Salt to taste

Mix the soup with ¼ cup of cold water and heat. Soak gelatin in ½ cup cold water and add to hot soup, stirring until gelatin is completely dissolved. Next add the cream cheese and stir briskly until smooth. While stirring in the cream cheese, do not allow mixture to boil. Remove from heat and add remaining ingredients. Place into a large mold, or individual molds, and cool in refrigerator until set. This makes an excellent summer meal which can be served with potato chips and a hearty green vegetable such as peas or beans. Serves 4.

Mock Lobster

1 cup crab meat, diced
1 cup shrimp, diced
1 can evaporated milk
  (13 oz. size)

2 slices fresh bread, crumbed
1 tablespoon butter
½ cup light cream
Salt and pepper to taste

6 buttered toast squares

Place all ingredients in the top of a double boiler and heat over simmering water. Do not boil. Serve hot over buttered toast. Serves 6.

Shellfish Casserole

½ pound crabmeat, cooked
½ pound lobster, cooked
1 pound shrimp,
  cooked and peeled
1 cup mayonnaise
½ cup chopped onion

½ cup green pepper, chopped
½ cup celery, chopped
2 cups cracker crumbs
2 tablespoons Worcestershire
  sauce
1 teaspoon salt

Pepper to taste

Combine all ingredients and place in a large casserole dish. Bake at 400° F. for 20 minutes. Serves 6 hungry persons quickly.

Fried Shellfish with Fruit

1 pound crab, lobster or   ¼ cup butter
   shrimp   Fruit or preserves of
½ cup flour   your choice
                Brown sugar

Rolls chunk of shellfish in flour and fry in butter until browned. Serve over a broiled peach or pear half sprinkled with brown sugar, or over chilled cranberry sauce or other preserve. This dish is exceptionally good over cooked pineapple slices with a pinch of lemon juice. Serves 2 to 4.

Shellfish Balls

½ cup butter   Salt and pepper to taste
2 tablespoons flour   ⅓ cup milk (approximate)
1 pound lobster, crabmeat
   or shrimp, minced

Cream butter until light, then stir in flour. Mix in the minced shellfish with a wooden spoon. Add seasonings and enough milk to bind the mixture together, but do not make it too soft.

Spoon dabs of the mixture into a well greased frying pan and fry on all sides until browned. Serve with tartar sauce or cocktail sauce. Serves 4.

Baked Shellfish Alaska

1 pound shellfish (any kind)   ½ cup onion, finely chopped
½ cup sour cream   Salt to taste
                ½ cup grated Parmesan cheese

Place raw shellfish in the bottom of a shallow, well-greased baking dish. Combine sour cream, onion, salt and cheese and spread over shellfish.

Bake at 350° F. until shellfish are tender. Garnish with paprika, season with pepper and serve piping hot. Serves 2 to 4.

Woods Hole Shellfish Casserole

1 pound shrimp,
  cooked and peeled
1 pound lobster, cooked
½ pound uncooked scallops
¼ cup butter

1 cup White Sauce
  (See Chapter Nine)
½ cup dry white wine
Bread crumbs
Greated Parmesan cheese

Saute raw scallops in butter for 5 minutes. Add lobster and shrimp meat cut into pieces the size of the scallops. Place in a casserole dish and cover with White Sauce and wine. Sprinkle the top with a layer of bread crumbs and a generous amount of grated cheese. Bake at 400° F. until browned (about 20 min.). Serves 6.

Shellfish Cucumber Boats

Shrimp, crabmeat or
  lobster (cooked)
Lettuce

Mayonnaise
Cucumbers

Mix any desired shellfish with enough mayonnaise to bind it together and season to taste. Cut a thin slice off the side of a whole cucumber and hollow out the center. Fill with shellfish mixture and place a leaf of lettuce in the center to look like a sail. Use a toothpick to support the sail.

Easy Texas Gumbo

¼ pound butter
1 pound okra
1 chopped onion
Salt and pepper to taste
3 tablespoons tomato paste

1 teaspoon thyme
1 garlic clove, chopped
½ pound crabmeat, cooked
½ pound shrimp,
  cooked and peeled
2 cups water

Melt butter in a large kettle and cook the okra and onion in it until tender. Season with salt and pepper. Add tomato paste, thyme, garlic, water and crab meat; boil for 15 minutes. Add shrimp and boil for 5 more minutes, stirring occasionally. Serves 6.

Lobster meat may be substituted for crab meat in this recipe with equally good results.

Shellfish Spread

¼ cup shrimp, cooked	3 tablespoons mayonnaise
¼ cup lobster, cooked	3 tablespoons Russian dressing
¼ cup crab meat, cooked	3 tablespoons cashew nuts, finely chopped

Mix together shellfish, mayonnaise, Russian dressing and chill. Spread on crackers or toast squares and top with crushed nuts. Makes approximately 1 cup.

Quick Shellfish Stew with Wine

1 pound cooked shellfish meat (Lobster, shrimp, or crab)	¼ cup butter
	¼ cup dry white wine
	1 quart light cream or milk
Salt and pepper to taste	

Cut shellfish into smallish chunks (about 1 inch squares) and set aside.

Pour milk or cream into top of a double boiler over boiling water. Add butter and seasonings and thoroughly heat the mixture, but do not boil. Add shellfish and wine and heat through (2 or 3 minutes). Serve hot in bowls topped with small crackers. Serves 4 to 6.

Chapter Nine

Recipes for Shellfish Sauces

THE FOLLOWING are recipes for the various shellfish sauces that have been mentioned throughout the text. They have been included here, in a chapter of their own, so as to save the endless repetition that would have resulted by including them with each and every recipe that calls for a particular sauce.

Cocktail Sauce Number One

4 tablespoons horseradish
1 dash Worcestershire
   sauce

4 tablespoons catsup
1 pinch salt
1 pinch cayenne pepper

Blend all the ingredients together and serve well chilled. This recipe will suffice as a dip for 1 dozen oysters, clams, or quahogs served on the half-shell.

Cocktail Sauce Number Two

½ teaspoon dry mustard
1 teaspoon lemon juice
1 cup catsup

1 teaspoon Worcestershire
sauce
Salt and pepper to taste

Dissolve the mustard in the lemon juice, add the remaining ingredients and mix well. Serve well chilled. This recipe will make about 1 cup.

Cocktail Sauce Number Three

2 tablespoons vinegar
2 tablespoons Worcestershire
sauce
4 tablespoons lemon juice

2 tablespoons horseradish
6 tablespoons catsup
1 teaspoon Tabasco sauce
½ teaspoon salt

Mix all ingredients together and serve well chilled. Makes 1 cup.

Medium-Thick White Sauce

2 tablespoons butter
2 tablespoons flour
1 cup milk

Melt butter in a saucepan over low heat. Add flour slowly and stir in well. Stir in milk a little at a time and cook over low heat, stirring constantly until thick and smooth. Makes 1 cup.

White Sauce

2 tablespoons butter
3 tablespoons flour

1 cup milk
¼ teaspoon salt
Pepper to taste

Heat the butter in a saucepan until it bubbles, then add flour and cook thoroughly. Lower the heat to the lowest possible flame and simmer. While simmering, add the milk a little at a time, stirring the mixture into a smooth paste each time it thickens. Lastly, add salt and pepper to taste. Makes about 1 cup.

Variations Using a Basic White Sauce

Cheese sauce: Add ½ cup grated cheese
Celery sauce: Add ⅓ to ½ cup finely chopped cooked celery
Mushroom sauce: Add ¼ to ½ cup chopped mushrooms

India Sauce

1 tablespoon butter	1 pinch pepper
1½ tablespoons flour	½ teaspoon curry powder
1 cup milk	3 tablespoons sweet pickles,
¼ teaspoon salt	finely chopped

Heat butter until it begins to bubble, then add flour and cook thoroughly. Allow mixture to slowly simmer over very low heat and slowly add in the milk, stirring the mixture to a smooth paste each time it thickens. Lastly, add salt, pepper, curry powder, and chopped pickles. Makes 1½ cups.

Left over fish and shellfish of all kinds will make an excellent meal when heated in this sauce.

Butter Sauce

3 tablespoons butter	1 teaspoon salt
1½ tablespoons flour	1 dash pepper

Place the butter in a cold saucepan and thoroughly mix the flour, salt, and pepper into it. Over this mixture pour a cup of boiling water. Cook for a few minutes, stirring constantly. Use immediately. Makes 1⅓ cups.

This sauce makes a great dip for crab meat, lobster, mussels, and steamed clams, or oysters.

Lemon Sauce

3 tablespoons sugar	1 lemon, wedged thin
1 cup milk	1 tablespoon butter

Place milk, sugar, and thin wedge of lemon into a saucepan and simmer gently for 10 minutes. Add juice of the lemon and the butter, stirring all gently until the butter has melted. Strain the sauce into dishes and use as soon as possible. Makes 1⅓ cups.

Tartar Sauce Number One

1 cup mayonnaise
1 teaspoon finely chopped
  onion
1 teaspoon finely chopped
  sweet pickles

1 teaspoon green olives,
  finely chopped
1 teaspoon parsley,
  finely chopped

Blend all the ingredients together and chill. This makes a great tartar sauce to use with any seafood you choose. Makes 1½ cups.

Tartar Sauce Number Two

1 cup mayonnaise
1 tablespoon lemon juice
Grated rind of 1 lemon

¼ cup onion, finely chopped
2 tablespoons green olives,
  finely chopped

Blend all ingredients together and chill before serving. Make 1½ cups.

Garlic Dip

½ cup butter
½ teaspoon garlic salt

Heat the butter until melted then stir in the garlic salt; use immediately. This is a great dip for steamed clams or oysters. Makes ½ cup.

Vinegar Sauce

The folks along the Gulf Coast of the United States use this fine sauce as a dip for oysters as well as for crayfish. To prepare this sauce, simply mix together the following ingredients:

½ cup vinegar
¼ teaspoon salt
1 dash cayenne pepper

Lobster Cocktail Sauce

⅓ cup mayonnaise   2 tablespoons lemon juice
1 pinch paprika   ¼ teaspoon salt

Combine all ingredients and chill in the refrigerator before using on lobster cocktails. Makes approximately ⅓ cup.

Hollandaise Sauce

½ cup butter   1 tablespoon wine vinegar
2 egg yolks   ½ teaspoon salt

Melt butter in the top of a double boiler. Add the remaining ingredients, stirring constantly until the mixture thickens. If you prefer a milder flavored sauce, use little less vinegar. Makes ¾ cup.

Ginger Sauce

¼ cup powdered ginger   ¼ cup soy sauce
⅓ cup sugar   ¼ cup white vinegar

Combine all ingredients and your sauce is ready. Makes 1¼ cups.
This makes a great topping for hot, fresh crab meat.

Hot Sauce

¼ cup soy sauce
1 teaspoon vegetable oil
2 tablespoons finely chopped hot peppers

Combine all ingredients and mix thoroughly.
This sauce makes a fine dip for steamed clams, mussels, or oysters for people who like hot stuff. Makes about ½ cup.

Dip for Shrimp

½ pound butter   ½ teaspoon Tabasco sauce

Juice of 2 lemons   ½ cup soy sauce

Melt butter in a saucepan, but do not allow it to reach the boiling point. Add remaining ingredients and blend well. Serve hot as a dip for plain boiled shrimp, crab or lobster. Makes 1½ cups.

Pizzaz Seafood Sauce

½ cup chili sauce
3 tablespoons lemon juice
2 tablespoons horseradish
4 drops Tabasco sauce

2 teaspoons Worcestershire
  sauce
1 dash cayenne pepper
Salt to taste

Combine all ingredients and chill thoroughly. This is an excellent sauce for dunking shrimp. Makes about ⅔ cup.

Wine Sauce for Shellfish

3 tablespoons butter
4 tablespoons flour
2 cups shellfish broth
  (clam, oyster, mussel)

2 egg yolks, beaten
3 tablespoons white wine
Salt and pepper to taste

Heat butter in a saucepan. Add flour and stir constantly until thick and smooth. Add broth slowly while cooking and stir for about 10 minutes. Lower heat and add egg yolks, but be careful not to allow the sauce to reach the boiling point again. Season to taste and add wine. Makes 2½ cups.

This is a delicious sauce to pour over any shellfish, and should be used as hot as possible. Excellent for dealing with leftovers.

Red Sauce

2 tablespoons onion, chopped
½ cup catsup

1 tablespoon Worcestershire
  sauce

3 tablespoons butter

Saute onion in butter, add catsup and Worcestershire sauce. Simmer all ingredients until heated through. Makes ¾ cups.

This sauce goes well over almost any plain boiled shellfish.

Butter-Cheese Sauce

½ cup melted butter
½ cup Cheddar cheese,
   grated
3 tablespoons catsup

1½ teaspoons horseradish
1 teaspoon lemon juice
1 dash garlic powder
Salt and pepper to taste

Combine all ingredients and blend well. Makes about 1¼ cups.

This sauce may be used to brush on any shellfish that are to be broiled, used as a dip for boiled shellfish, or simply poured over cooked shellfish to make a complete dish.

Lobster Shell Butter

1 pound lobster shells
¼ cup butter

1 pinch salt and pepper
½ cup water

Dry the shells from a few cooked lobsters in a warm oven for 15 to 20 minutes. Crush shells and mix with butter and seasonings in a saucepan. Add water and simmer gently for 25 minutes. Strain shells from mixture; and place mixture in refrigerator to cool (approximately 30-40 minutes). Spoon the butter from the top of the cooled mixture, discard remaining liquid and remelt the butter for use as a dip for any boiled shellfish. Makes approximately 1 cup.

Noe: Shrimp shells may be treated in the same manner to produce an equally good tasting butter dip.

Honey Sauce

½ cup butter, melted
2 tablespoons blackberry
   brandy

1 tablespoon lemon juice
1 tablespoon honey

Combine all ingredients and serve as a dip for boiled shellfish. This sauce should be served hot and is certain to be a big hit with those who enjoy something different. Makes ¾ cups.

Normandy Sauce

4 tablespoons butter

4 tablespoons flour

4 cups shellfish liquor
(broth or juice)

1 cup light cream, beaten

4 egg yolks

Salt and pepper to taste

Melt butter in a saucepan over low heat. Add flour and stir until thick and brown. Gradually add 2 cups of the shellfish liquor (clam, mussel or oyster), stirring constantly until thick and smooth. Reduce heat to the simmering point and add remaining liquor and seasonings to taste. Simmer 30 minutes, stirring occasionally.

When ready to serve, add beaten cream with 4 egg yolks and heat over very low flame (do not allow to boil). Makes 6 cups.

This sauce is delicious when poured over steamed oysters, mussels or clams.

Chapter Ten

Miscellaneous Shellfish

IT WOULD, of course, be impossible within the confines of this book to go into details about all the various edible shellfish available as food for mankind. However, I shall attempt to cover in this chapter some of the most important shellfish which are readily available to the seashore forager, and describe some ways in which they can be cooked and eaten.

ABALONE

The abalone, which is really a large sea snail measuring up to a foot in diameter, is found only on parts of the Pacific coast of the U.S., but mainly in Mexican, Hawaiian, and Californian waters. The firm, white "foot" (which abalone hunters must pry loose from the rocks with crowbars) is a delicious meat and makes up the major portion of the abalones contents. However, in order to turn fresh abalone meat into mouth watering consistency, it must be tenderized first.

Japanese immigrants, who were extremely fond of abalone, first opened the eyes of Americans to the culinary possibilities of this once common and despised shellfish, found all along California's offshore rocks. The result of American preference for abalone flesh is that abalone steaks fetch about four dollars per pound and are becoming quite scarce. This scarcity continues despite strict California laws against shipping fresh abalone out of the state, in effect since 1915, as well as laws limiting the size and number of abalones that may be taken by commercial or private gatherers.

The abalone has a thin, oval, elongated shell with an outer surface of a dull, uniform brownish color with spiral undulations. The inner surface of the shell consists of a high-grade mother-of-pearl, which is a beauty to behold. The central muscle, which is a large foot used to cling to rocks and move about, is the edible portion and resembles a giant scallop removed from its shell.

To prepare abalone for cooking, remove from its shell and trim off all soft and dark portions. Beat the remaining meat vigorously with a wooden mallet, or regular hammer, until it becomes soft, but not mushy. Normally several abalone steaks are required for a meal for two.

Cooking Abalone

You can simply toast any plain old tenderized abalone steak under the broiler for a few minutes and salt to taste.

Another method is to cut the meat up into half-inch pieces, after tenderizing, and soak them in a cup of wine (dry sherry is best) for 15 minutes. Wipe dry after soaking, dip each chunk into 2 well beaten eggs, and then into seasoned cracker crumbs. Fry in butter for a minute or two on each side and serve with lime juice squeezed over the top. Never cook abalone for prolonged periods. It will result in re-toughening the meat. Abalone can only stand a very few minutes of cooking by any heat source or cooking method.

Canned abalone is available in most parts of the U.S. and is very simple to use. Most cans contain about a pound of meat, and once opened, the meat can be stored safely in the refrigerator for a week or so, if placed in a jar with a tight fitting lid, and covered with its own juice. Abalone is always tenderized and trimmed for eating prior to the canning process. It needs no further treatment, and may be eaten straight from the can, for example in a salad, or may be very briefly cooked in any way that you might like. One can usually contains about six whole abalone steaks, a sufficient amount to serve four people.

Broiled Abalone Steaks

1 pound abalone steaks	1 dash paprika
4 tablespoons butter	3 tablespoons mayonnaise

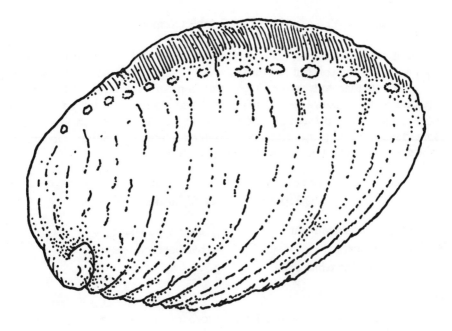

ABALONE SHELL

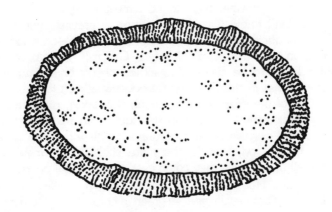

ABALONE MEAT
(Trim away shaded portion)

¼ teaspoon salt   1 tablespoon lemon juice

Cut abalone steaks into ½ inch thick slices and tenderize by beating with a mallet until soft but not mushy.

Mix together salt, lemon juice, and paprika in a bowl and marinate abalone in the mixture for 20 minutes. Place steaks on a broiler pan and cook a few inches below the broiler flame at 400° F. Cook 5 minutes, turn, spread with mayonnaise and cook another 5 minutes. Serve hot with a tablespoon of melted butter poured over the top. Serves 4.

Japanese Sweet Abalone

1 pound abalone meat   2 tablespoons sugar
1 cup water   1 tablespoon soy sauce
3 tablespoons white wine
  (dry)

Place abalone meat into a large saucepan and add the water. Bring to a full boil, then lower heat and simmer for 10 minutes. Add the wine and sugar and cook for 5 additional minutes; then stir in soy sauce and cook 3 minutes more. Cool, then cut abalone slices ½ inch thick and serve. Serves 2.

CRAYFISH

Crayfish are a gourmet treat found almost everywhere in the United States. If you don't know them by the name of crayfish, you might know them by one of their various other common names—crawdad, crawfish, freshwater crab, or freshwater lobster. Crayfish has a very delicate flavor, which I find to be superior to either lobster or shrimp. It is rarely found on the market in the U.S., except occasionally on the west coast and in certain areas of the deep south. It abounds in lakes, rivers, and swampy areas, being particularly abundant in the south and midwest. I have even occasionally found crayfish in ponds around the New England states and in Canada. On Cape Cod, though, there are shellfish gourmets who know where to find all the crayfish they could ever want in local ponds.

You will have little difficulty in recognizing a crayfish the first time you spot one. They are usually grayish-green in color, from 3 to 6 inches long, and look very much like a small lobster, although they are mostly all tail. They can be found in anything from a few inches to a few feet of water (fresh or slightly brackish) and often in no water at all. They quite commonly make burrows along the side of streams and ponds, and often lie at the mouths of their holes in wait for passing prey. They are chiefly nocturnal, feeding mainly at night upon insects, mollusks, dead animals, etc.

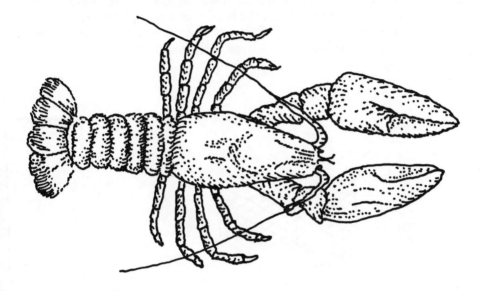

CRAYFISH

Catching Crayfish

There are several ways to catch crayfish, all of which are basically simple. When you go "crawfishin," try to catch as large a quantity as possible—it takes a great many crayfish to make a respectable meal; 40 to 60 should do nicely.

Look carefully for crayfish, and you will find them in such places as drainage ditches, under rocks, under logs, in mud holes, etc. Once located, it's simply a matter of picking them up. Be careful of their claws though, they can pinch hard enough to draw blood from an unwary finger.

Another method of catching the scrumptious crayfish, either on land or in the water, is to tie a small chunk of meat (bacon works well) onto the end of a string and dangle it in the water, or in front of their land burrows. The crayfish is tenacious when it gets hold of something to eat and you can gently pull him within range of a dip net without his being any the wiser until too late.

I like to catch crayfish with a simple trap, similar to a home made minnow trap. This can be made from any large jar with a fairly wide mouth as follows:

(1) Rig up a funnel over the mouth of your jar (see illustration).
(2) Place some bait inside the jar (meat scraps, bacon, bread crusts, etc.) and lower the jar into the bottom of a pond, lake, or stream.
(3) Leave your trap overnight (remember that crayfish are mainly nocturnal), and check your traps in the morning.

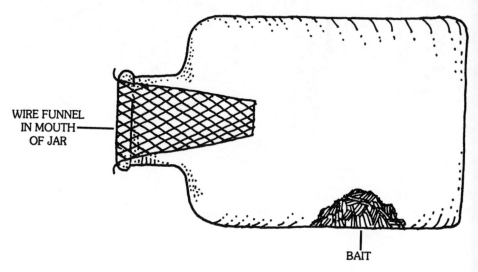

WIRE FUNNEL
IN MOUTH
OF JAR

BAIT

CRAYFISH TRAP
(2 quart wide mouthed jar)

Cooking Crayfish

The best method of preparing crayfish is to first "de-vein" and, then boil them. To "de-vein," grasp them by the middle section of the tail and pull with a twisting motion. The vein will pull right out. Boil the whole crayfish for about 10 minutes in salted water (2 tablespoons salt to 1 quart water). When cool enough to handle, peel off the shells and legs and cut off the heads at the first joint. The meat is then ready to be chilled for cocktails, prepared in any recipe calling for crayfish, or used as a substitute in any recipe calling for shrimp, prawns, or lobster. It can also be frozen for later use.

Crayfish New Orleans

3 tablespoons butter	1 teaspoon salt
1 large onion, chopped	½ teaspoon thyme
2 stalks celery, chopped	1 dash Tabasco sauce
3 large tomatoes, diced	1 cup cooked rice
40 crayfish	

Melt butter in a large frying pan and brown the onion and celery, adding a dash of salt and pepper. Add tomatoes to mixture in frying pan. Allow to simmer with just a touch of water until the tomatoes become soft. Add Tabasco sauce, rice, thyme, and crayfish. Cover and simmer for 10 additional minutes. Serve hot. Serves 6.

Crayfish Marinère

2 tablespoons butter	½ teaspoon pepper
3 dozen crayfish, cleaned	1½ cups white wine (dry)
1 finely chopped onion	3 tablespoons parsley,
1½ teaspoons salt	chopped

Melt butter in a frying pan and saute the crayfish until they turn a reddish color. Add onion, salt, pepper, and wine. Cover and cook over a low heat for 10 minutes. Take a sample taste for seasonings and add more if you like. Sprinkle with parsley and serve hot. Serves 4.

Crayfish for a Crowd

The following is a French recipe for crayfish that I think you will enjoy. Crayfish have been a source of food in France, as well as other European countries, for centuries. In fact, the French have even gone to the extent of farming crayfish on a commercial basis.

4 cups water	50 crayfish
1½ teaspoons salt	8 slices stale bread
¼ teaspoon black pepper	8 cups crayfish stock
1 onion, diced	¼ cup white wine
1 stalk celery, diced	4 tablespoons butter

Bouquet garni (4 sprigs parsley, 1 sprig thyme, and a bay leaf
tied inside a little cheesecloth bag)

Dice the celery and onion and add to water with salt, pepper, and bouquet garni. Bring mixture to a rolling boil and add crayfish. Lower heat and simmer for 15 minutes. Strain off the liquid and set aside for the moment. You may also now dispose of the bouquet garni. When crayfish are cool enough to handle, clean and extract the meat from the tails. Add enough water to the juice that was first set aside, to make 8 cups. Place this stock back on the stove over a gentle heat and add the stale bread. Stir until the bread and stock are well blended. Add the wine and bring to a boil, stirring constantly. Just before serving, place in the crayfish meat and add the butter. This dish should be served immediately while as hot as possible. Serves 6 to 8.

Crayfish in Court Bouillon

2 cups white wine	1 bay leaf
2 cups water	2 cloves garlic
1 onion, finely chopped	3 sprigs parsley
1 carrot, finely chopped	Salt and pepper to taste

50 crayfish, cleaned

Prepare a court bouillon of wine, water, onion, carrot, bayleaf, garlic, parsley, and salt and pepper. Combine these ingredients and simmer for about 30 minutes. Add crayfish to the bouillon and simmer (do not boil) for another 10 minutes. Serve crayfish hot and eat like lobster. Be sure to remove the black vein from the center of each crayfish tail as you eat it.

A delightful dip for crayfish can be made by combining ¼ pound melted butter with ¼ teaspoon paprika and a dash of salt. Serves 6.

Crayfish Bisque

50 crayfish	2 tablespoons flour
2 quarts water	¾ cup celery, finely chopped
2 onions, finely chopped	1 pinch of thyme
2 tablespoons butter	Salt and pepper to taste

Place crayfish into a large kettle with the water and boil for 10 to 15 minutes. Strain, and save the water. Pick the meat from all the crayfish and set aside for the moment.

Return empty shells to the water in which they were originally boiled, and cook for 30 minutes over a low heat. Fry onions in the butter and add the flour, cooking until browned over a low flame. Strain the boiling mixture containing the shells into the butter and onion mixture, stirring well. Add celery and crayfish meat. Season mixture with salt and pepper to taste, simmer for 15 minutes, then serve as hot as possible. Serves 6.

Creamed New England Crayfish

1 cup Medium-thick White Sauce (See Chapter Nine)
15 to 20 precooked crayfish, shelled
1 dash dry white wine

Add the crayfish meat and a dash of wine to the Medium-thick White Sauce. Heat in an oven until hot and serve. Serves 2.

Pickled Crayfish

2 cups vinegar
1 tablespoon dry mustard
1 pound raw crayfish,
    shelled and deveined

1 tablespoon cayenne pepper
½ teaspoon celery salt
3 bay leaves

Place all of the ingredients except crayfish in a saucepan and bring to a boil. Add the raw crayfish and boil for 15 minutes. Crayfish are done when they can be pierced easily with a fork. Place in a clean glass jar, cover with the seasoned vinegar mix, seal, and store in the refrigerator. These pickled crayfish will keep for a long time and will improve with age. Serves 2.

GEODUCKS

The geoduck clam (Panope generosa) is by far the largest of the American bivalves found within the intertidal zone, and is very highly regarded for its edible qualities. The geoduck resembles the ordinary soft-shelled clam in its physical make up, but is about ten times larger in size. Geoducks up to 10 inches in length, weighing many pounds are not uncommon. In years past, before these giant clams were so pitifully reduced in their numbers, many were known to be even larger.

Hunting for geoducks, or "gooeyducking" as this sport is called in the Pacific Northwest where geoducks are found, is a fascinating adventure requiring more than a little hard work and tenacity. These virtues are required because this giant clam lives deep down in sandy-mud, and by deep I mean really deep: 3 to 6 feet beneath the surface. It takes a major excavation project to uncover a geoduck. If you have ever tried digging a three foot deep hole in the sand, close to the water's edge, with the sides constantly sluffing in, you will appreciate the task involved in digging up just one geoduck.

If you are going out in search of geoducks for the first time, it would be best to team up with someone who knows the ropes. It takes an expert to tell the difference between the vent holes made in the sand by geoducks, and those made by other clams dwelling in the same area which are very similar in appearance. In addition, a two man team is often required to accomplish the sometimes long and strenuous task of digging up a geoduck.

Most geoducks are found on mud flats located just to seaward of the average low tide line. This means that the only time it will pay off to hunt geoducks is during periods of extra low, or minus tides. It is only at these times that the mud flats will be sufficiently uncovered to permit you to dig large holes upon them.

Assuming that you have located the burrow of a geoduck, your next problem will be how to dig him out. The most popular method is to speedily remove a few shovelsful of mud, until the sides of your excavation appear to be in danger of caving in. At this point shove a wide stove pipe down into the soft mud, directly over the spot where the geoduck should be. By using a dipper, you can bail out the mud from inside the stove pipe, which will allow you to continue shoving the pipe further down into the mud. Eventually you should be able to shove your arm down the stove pipe, firmly grasp the geoduck, and haul it out by force. Don't use a stove pipe any longer than the length of your arm. The geoduck will not burrow any deeper than the length of his siphon (3 to 6 feet), so don't worry about disturbing him for fear that he will burrow beyond all possible reach. The geoduck's main defense is the firm hope that you will give up your efforts in disgust before you reach his deep lair.

If you are unable to reach the geoduck through the stove pipe, you might have to dig a large hole to one side of the stove pipe to get at him. To accomplish this process in soft mud, it will take a two man team, working at a feverish clip. One worker should do the shovel work while the other rapidly bails out the watery mud and sand constantly threatening to fill in the hole.

Geoducks make grand steaks when the thick mantle portion is thinly sliced and fried in butter. The large siphons are usually cooked, skinned, and then diced for use in stews and chowders. You may use any clam chowder recipe and simply substitute chopped geoduck meat for clam meat.

The limit on a geoduck catch is three per day per person in the State of Washington. However, three of these giant clams, which may weigh up to 10 pounds each, will provide several meals for a large sized family. Geoducks are found in greatest numbers in the Puget Sound area, in the State of Washington. They may also be found on occasion along the Oregon coast and in extreme northern California waters.

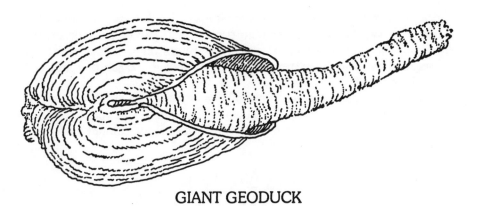

GIANT GEODUCK

SEA URCHINS

The sea urchins are members of the Echinoderm Family, thus being directly related to sand dollars and star fish. There are several varieties of sea urchins commonly found along the shoreline which, although avoided like the plague by bathers along rocky shores, are quite delicious to eat. They contain no edible flesh, but do contain a rich roe, a highly prized food rivaling the finest caviar. Sea urchins cling to rocks, sometimes in great clusters, at the low-tide line, or a bit lower, and are found along both coasts of the U.S. They appear almost spherical in shape and are covered with many long spines and therefore must be gathered cautiously with tongs or gloved hands.

The most common sea urchins found along our shores are: The Green Urchin, a short spined creature of about 2 to 2½ inches in diameter which is stuck with the longest two-word Latin name in zoology, Strongylocentaotus drobachiensis; the Purple Urchin (Arbacia punctulata), found along the entire Atlantic and Gulf coasts, which is 1 to 2 inches in diameter with longer but duller spines that the Green Urchin; the Giant Urchin of the Pacific coast (Strongylocentaotus franciscanus), which is often as large as 6 inches in diameter and found all along the Pacific coast from Alaska southwards. This large urchin is reputed to be the finest eating of all.

Sea urchins are best gathered during the season extending from midsummer through mid-winter to insure the best roe. During this season you may gather an occasional specimen with little or no roe at all, or perhaps some with a tiny amount of pale white, dried out roe. Sea urchins are easy enough to collect, as they do not fight and are incapable of running away. You may simply pick them off the rocks to which they cling during low tide and toss them into a basket for later cleaning. Don't forget to bring along a pair of gloves, you'll need them to protect your hands from the urchin's sharp spines. Urchins living in temperate waters do not have poisonous spines but they can fester up a dandy sore spot if you jab one into your finger. Be careful!

As I have mentioned, sea urchins have little flesh to speak of, their appeal being the delicate coral roe sought by gourmets. This roe, located just beneath the top of the rounded shell, is a bright orange colored mass easily

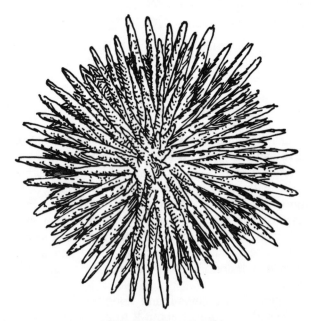

SPINY SEA URCHIN

removed with a spoon once the urchin is cut in half. It takes many sea urchins to obtain a little roe, but this rich tasting material is satisfying in relatively small amounts.

The roe of sea urchins is never cooked, but eaten raw. It can be served on the half-shell, so to speak, whereupon the diner simply scoops out the roe with a spoon, sprinkles it with salt and a squeeze of lemon juice, and eats it with an accompaniment of a chilled white wine. A great dip for crackers or chips can be made from the following recipe.

Sea Urchin Dip

1 cup cottage cheese   ¼ cup sea urchin roe

Force the roe through a sieve and thoroughly mix with cottage cheese. This is a dynamite dip that will convert even the most finicky eaters to sea urchin roe.

THE CONCHS

Conch is a common name widely applied to a large number of marine snails found in all oceans of the world. In the United States the term is generally used to denote members of the Strombus family.

The flesh of the large pink queen conch (Strombus gigas) is commonly used for bait, as well as for a source of food in Florida, the Caribbean and the Bahamas. In these areas the conch is a food item of great commercial value, and is often found on the menus of better restaurants in the Miami area.

Various species of the conch, including the edible helmet shells, are found from North Carolina southward, including all of the Gulf coast area. They can be found within the intertidal area, but more often are located in deeper waters. Conchs may be gathered by wading about in shallow waters or upon sand bars. Much better results can be had by setting baited traps for them in deeper water, where wading is impossible.

An effective trap can be made from an old automobile tire (see illustration) with a circle of wire screen attached to one side to prevent losing the catch as you haul up the trap. The bait should be placed into a ball of coarse wire to protect it from fish, or immediate destruction by crabs also present in the area. The bait should be attached securely to the center of the trap. Meat scraps, fish heads, etc. make effective bait; the riper the better. Attach four ropes or wires to the tire to form a bridle to which a rope reaching up to the surface is attached. For best results, lower the trap into the water in early evening and haul it up early the next morning. You won't catch any queen conch with this trap as they are not carnivorous, but you will attract other conchs, as well as helmet shells, whelks and perhaps a crab or lobster if you're lucky.

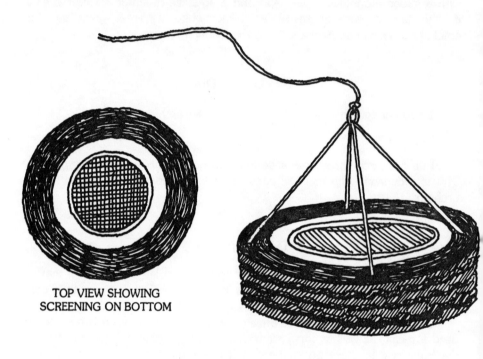

TOP VIEW SHOWING
SCREENING ON BOTTOM

CONCH AND WHELK TRAP

To prepare conchs for eating, they must be opened and the meat removed. This is most easily accomplished by hammering off the conical tip of the shell, to provide easy access to the meat so that it may be removed without fuss. In the Caribbean, the natives hang conchs upside down, by the foot, on a nail which allows the animal to gently slip out of its shell within 24 hours or so. I don't recommend this method at all—it's a rather odiferous operation and quite messy. I suspect the natives employ this method in order to save the colorful shells, which are in demand for the tourist trade.

Conch Chowder

1 cup conch meat, finely chopped	1 stalk celery, diced
2½ cups water	1 small potato, diced
1 carrot, sliced	1 pinch thyme and oregano
	Salt and pepper to taste

Boil the chopped conch meat in 2½ cups of salted water for 25 to 30 minutes. Add carrots, celery, potatoes, and seasonings. Simmer until vegetables are tender then serve hot. Serves 2.

Used in any chowder recipe, you will find the conch a strong rival of clams, quahogs, or surf clams as an excellent chowder shellfish. To tenderize chopped conch meat, boil in salted water for about a half hour before use as an ingredient in chowders, stews, or soups. This practice holds true of all the conch varieties including the helmet shells.

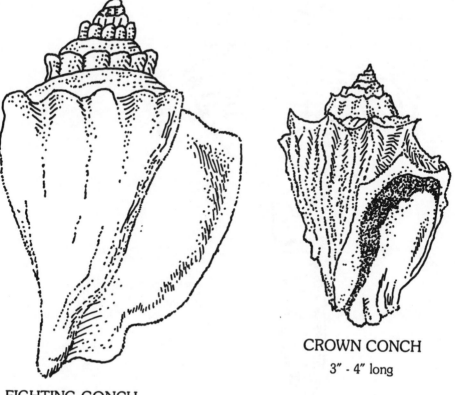

FIGHTING CONCH
2″ to 5″ long

CROWN CONCH
3″ - 4″ long

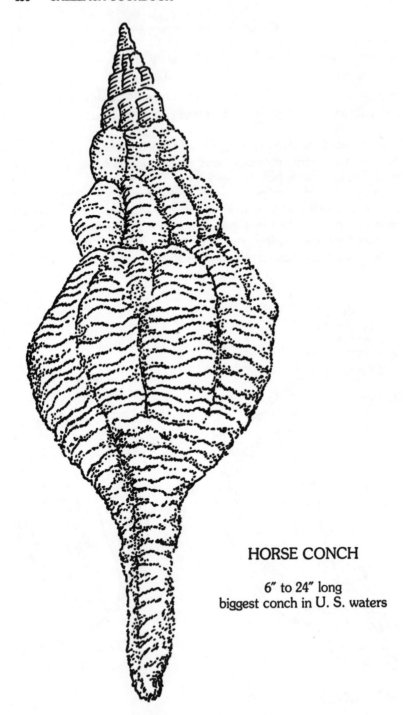

HORSE CONCH

6″ to 24″ long
biggest conch in U. S. waters

Salad Material

In the Antilles, conchs are diced, marinated in lime juice for several hours, and added raw to tossed green salads.

Deep Fried Conch

Boil whole pieces of conch meat in salted water for 30 minutes. Remove from water and further tenderize by beating with a hammer or meat tenderizing mallet. Don't just peck at them with the hammer —beat them unmercifully and with a will.

Prepare an egg batter and dip meat, cut into ½ inch squares, then roll in fine bread or cracker crumbs. Deep fry in hot fat until golden brown. Serve hot with tartar sauce.

It is claimed that the high copper content of the conch is responsible for the low incidence of copper-deficiency anemia and poliomyelitis among the Bahamians. Indeed conch is a popular food item in the Bahamas, second only to the spiny lobster in economic importance to the Nassau fishing fleet.

THE TINY COQUINA CLAM

The coquina or wedge shell (Donax) is a little known member of the edible clam family. The reason for this is probably because of their small size (½ inch to 1 inch in length) which tends to confuse those who have heard that they are edible, but can't figure out how to make a meal from the infinitesimally small amount of meat contained in each tiny clam. It is not, however, the meat of these clams which concerns the shellfish gourmet, but rather the smooth tasting, superior broth which can be prepared from them.

The four most popular varieties of the coquina clam are: The Bean clams (Donas gouldii and Donax californicus), found along the sand beaches of the west coast of the U.S., most numerous in southern California; the Coquina clam (Donax variabilis), an east coast species found from southern Virginia all the way around to the Texas Gulf coast; and the Digger Wedge (Donax fossor), found from the southern shores of New England southwards to Florida, most abundant in the southern states.

The small size of the coquina clam is more than balanced by the vast numbers normally found within a small area of their colonies. It is not uncommon to find upwards of one thousand within an area of 2 or 3 square feet. Thus, it is not much trouble to gather a pail full in 15 or 20 minutes by simply sifting them from the sand with a wire screen, or a kitchen sieve.

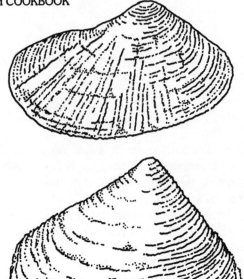

COQUINA SHELLS

½″ to 1¼″

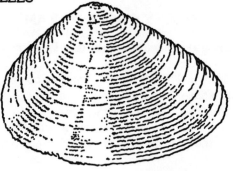

Coquinas are found on sandy beaches between the areas of mid-tide and the low-tide line, also on bars that are awash or exposed at low tide. Their colonies are easily spotted by looking for the thousands of tiny holes that they make in the sand. You will often spot these holes running in a long narrow strip down the beach. They are a dead giveaway of a thriving coquina bed. Look for these holes just after a wave has washed across the beach and receded back to the water line. You won't see the holes as the waves wash over them and saturate the sand, but they will show up plainly just after the wave has receded, prior to the next wave.

The more crowded the coquina colony is, and the longer between waves, the better to spot their holes. Once you have worked it out for yourself, you will always be able to easily recognize a bed of coquinas.

Having located a colony or "bed" of coquinas, all you will need is a shovel and some sort of device to sift sand from the shells contained in each shovelful. Coquinas cannot burrow very deeply (only an inch or so) so little hard work is involved in their gathering. Keep shoveling and sifting until you have gathered the amount you need (about ½ gallon for the recipes which follow).

HOW TO BUILD A COQUINA SIEVE

If you are digging coquinas in an area where they are not overly plentiful, you might want to build a sieve, and let the waves wash your sand effortlessly for you as you shovel it into this sieve. This set up will save you a lot of the work in sifting each shovelful, and allow you to devote most of your time to digging.

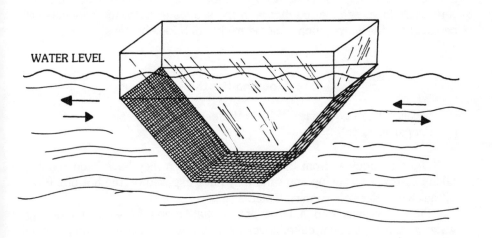

WATER LEVEL

COQUINA SEIVE

Build a box similar to that shown in the illustration and set it on the beach lengthwise, in a location where the waves will wash through it.

The sloping ends and bottom are made of fine meshed screen which allows the waves to pass through and automatically wash the contents.

If you should find that you are digging in an area where there is a high ratio of dead shells to live ones, you will find it too time consuming to sort them out by hand. However, there is a way of getting rid of the unwanted empties by taking advantage of the natural behavior of the coquina.

To employ this little known method, empty your sieve of mixed live and dead shells into the bottom of a large pail. Next fill the pail with sand, almost to the top. Add enough sea water to completely saturate the sand and bring the level to an inch above the top of the sand. Give the contents of the pail a vigorous stir with your hand until the coquinas, sand, and water are all in suspension and moving. After you have gotten everything moving well, stop and let it sit for a minute or two. As you stirred the mixture, the dead shells will have settled to the bottom and the live ones will have risen to the top. Scoop off the top layer of sand, and with it will come all of the live coquinas. Place them back in your sieve and rinse them of all loose sand.

After rinsing off the batch of pure coquinas, place in a bucket containing enough clean sea water to cover them. In a short while they will open up and purge themselves of any sand and grit that may have gotten inside them. Don't place them into fresh water, or a salted fresh water solution. If you do, they will close up tightly, for good, and will probably die in a very short time. After a few hours in the sea water bath, the coquinas will be ready for the preparation of some mighty delicious broth:

Coquina Broth

½ gallon fresh coquinas   Water
Pepper to taste

Dip the coquinas from the sea water in which they have been soaking, taking care not to stir up any sand they have expelled on the bottom. Rinse off quickly under cold running water.

Place coquinas into a large pot or kettle and fill with just enough water to almost, but not quite, cover them. Cover the pot and bring to a full rolling boil. Lower heat and simmer for 15 minutes. Pour off the broth and serve hot. Discard the coquina shells. You may season the broth with pepper, but will probably find that the natural salt content of this broth is sufficent without adding more. Serves 6.

Donax Nectar

½ gallon fresh coquinas   1 cup white wine

2½ cups water   Butter

1 dash of garlic salt

Boil the coquinas for 15 minutes in a covered kettle containing water, wine, and garlic salt. Pour off the broth and serve with a dab of butter floating on the top of each bowl of steaming nectar. Serves 6.

The use of any of the varieties of coquina clam as a broth in clam stews or clam soup recipes, will give that dish an unparalleled taste. It will be your secret ingredient that will keep even the experts guessing. There is simply no finer broth to be had than that which is prepared from these tiny coquina clams.

THREE LESSER KNOWN CRABS

Perhaps I should have included these three types of crabs in the crab section of this book, but I felt that they were unique enough to be discussed in a place of their own.

Hermit Crab—

The hermit crab is a rather odd little fellow. He is classed as a Crustacean and belongs to a very small but very common group. This fellow can be found in shallow waters, as well as scurrying along beaches throughout the entire world. The hermit crabs are unique in that they have no shell of their own. They must hunt up the abandoned shells of mollusks or other items, such as beer cans, etc., to use as homes and protective coverings for their soft and vulnerable bodies. As they grow larger, they discard their borrowed shells and move into larger homes in a bigger shell.

Hermit crabs are scavengers, a habit they share with their cousins the hard-shelled crabs. They can be easily identified by their soft, curved abdomens with hook-like tails, and their rather attractive pinkish-orange coloration. They are commonly about 1 to 5 inches in length.

When cooked, the entire portion of these soft crabs is edible. They can be cooked in many of the same ways that regular crabs are cooked, or cleaned, returned to their borrowed shells and roasted in a hot oven for about 15 minutes.

Oyster Crabs (Pea crab)

The oyster crab (Pinnotheres ostreum) is a tiny little crab with a soft

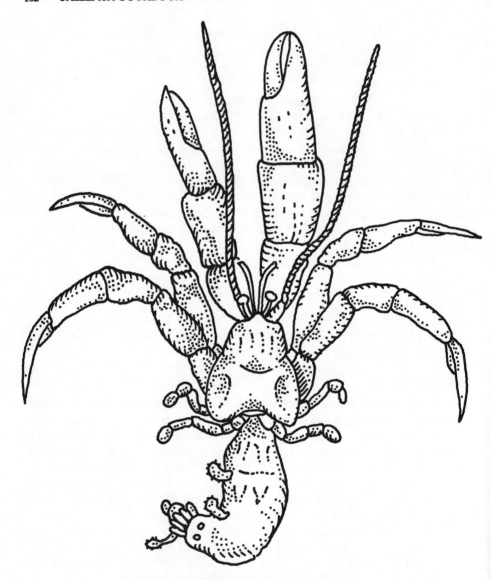

A HERMIT CRAB WITHOUT SHELL

shell which lives inside of the shells of live oysters, and depends upon the oysters' shell for protection. This is a very delicately flavored crab much sought after by gourmets. Unfortunately, the supply of oyster crabs is limited to the numbers you might find while shucking your own supply of freshly caught oysters. It might be possible to gather a supply from a commercial oyster packing house, if you let them know that you are in the market for them.

Properly prepared, the oyster crab is a simply delicious dish, so I include the following recipe, which, I sincerely hope you will try, should you ever run across a batch of them in sufficient numbers to make a meal.

Fried Oyster Crabs

4 dozen oyster crabs   ½ cup sifted flour
  (or whatever you can get)   Salt and pepper
           Cooking oil to cover

Rinse crabs quickly under cold running water and dry on absorbent towels. Roll them in flour and sprinkle with salt and pepper. Place a few at a time into hot, deep fat and fry until browned. Drain and serve with tartar sauce. The entire crab is edible—just pop them into your mouth whole Serves 2.

Mussel Crabs—

The so-called American mussel crab (Pinnotheres maculatus) is a little crab commonly found living inside of the blue mussel, and occasionally in other bivalves. This little greenish-colored scamp is a cousin of the oyster crab, and has the same soft shell and size, usually less than an inch across at the widest point.

The mussel crab is equally as delicately flavored as the oyster crab, and can be prepared for eating in the same way. As with oyster crabs, they are entirely edible, each one being a bite sized delicacy you won't soon forget.

MOON SHELL SNAILS

Moon shells are another example of those common gastropods, which are not only edible, but as delicious as its cousins the conchs, whelks, and abalones. The northern moon shell, which grows up to 5 inches in diameter, is the largest and best known of the species. Moon shell, however, and its closely related kin the nautica shells, are found along all hard packed sandy beaches of the Atlantic and Pacific oceans.

Moon shells are opened and prepared for eating in the same ways that the conchs and whelks are treated, so I will let you work out your own recipes for them instead of adding some here, which would be merely space wasting variations on the same theme.

Incidentally, the meat of conchs, whelks and moon shells is much improved by freezing for several weeks prior to being prepared as food. It seems that aging them in the freezer makes for a vastly more tender product. To freeze, remove the meat from the shells and cut it into small cubes or steaks; then wrap well and freeze raw.

TWO VARIETIES OF MOON SHELL SNAILS

WHELKS

Among the many species of whelks, the two most important as food items are the channeled whelk and the knobbed whelk (Bustcon canaliculatum and B. carica). These are found from the Canadian Maritime Provinces southwards along the Atlantic coast, and also along the entire shoreline of the Gulf of Mexico. The knobbed whelk is the largest gastropod found in northern waters and, as its name would suggest, it can be easily recognized by its knobby, brownish-colored exterior. The channeled whelk is almost the equal of the knobbed whelk in size and has the same coloration, but has a slightly softer shell. The waved whelk (Buccinum undatum) is another of the common whelks, and is as edible as any other species.

Whelks can be gathered in much the same manner as conchs, using the automobile tire trap described in that section. Whelks are carnivorous creatures and spend most of their time actively crawling around on the bottom. Whelks are also easily gathered in shallow water areas, by simply wading around and picking them up. Search beaches right after an exceptionally high storm surf has settled down, and you may find lots of live whelks washed up on the beach or in shallow water in the process of retreating back from whence they came.

Removing the meat from a whelk is a simple process. Just give the shell a gentle tap with a hammer, or similar blunt instrument, and crack it open. Remove the meat and rinse it under cold water to rid the meat of any bits of broken shell.

Whelk Steaks

Steaks can be sliced from the body and big muscular foot portions of all types of whelks. Each of these steaks must, however, undergo a tenderizing process prior to frying, baking, or broiling. Cut into ½ inch to ¾ inch slices and pound with a hammer until soft but not mushy. You will find them quite tasty just rolled in seasoned flour and fried in a skillet.

Whelk Chowder

2 pounds whelk meat, shucked	¼ teaspoon oregano
½ pound bacon	¼ teaspoon tarragon
2 onions, sliced	¼ teaspoon marjoram
4 medium potatoes, diced	Salt to taste
½ teaspoon pepper	2 cups milk
	½ cup cream

Put whelk meat through a chopper or meat grinder and chop until very fine pieces are obtained.

Cut bacon into small bits and fry in the bottom of a kettle until almost crisp. Remove and set aside for the moment.

Add onions to the kettle and fry in the bacon fat until soft; then remove and set aside with the bacon.

Cover the whelk meat and potatoes with hot water and cook until potatoes are almost done. Return onion and bacon to the kettle. Add milk, cream, and seasonings and bring just to the boiling point, but do not allow to boil or the milk will curdle. Serve hot topped with small crackers. Serves 4 to 6.

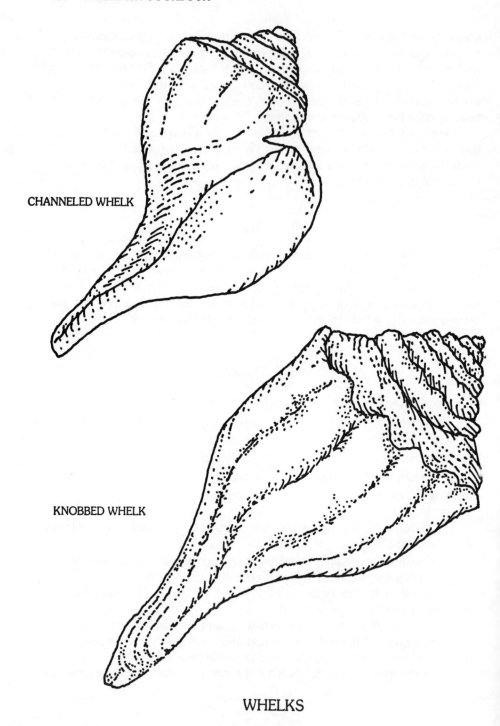

CHANNELED WHELK

KNOBBED WHELK

WHELKS

PERIWINKLES

There are over a dozen common species of periwinkles spread along both the Atlantic and Pacific shorelines of the U.S. Periwinkles are actually small snails, usually of a brownish color, varying in size from about ½ inch to 1½ inches in size.

The most common periwinkle 'is called just that, the common periwinkle (Littorina littorea). They are easily collected along most rocky coastlines in the intertidal area. Many thousands will be exposed during low tide in a good periwinkle collecting area. It is no trouble at all to collect quite a few in no time at all.

All sea snails are edible, but the periwinkle of the littorina family are especially good and have a delicately flavored meat which is agreeable to any common shellfish lover. Periwinkles are considered in season all year with no one time being better than another to partake of this delicacy.

The most common way to prepare the different varieties of periwinkles for eating, is to boil them in salted water for 20 minutes, then serve them hot in the shell. They are to be extracted with the aid of a stout pin or seafood fork, dipped in melted butter and then devoured whole. Periwinkles can also be roasted in their shells and then served and eaten in the same manner as with the boiled ones. Roasting should take about 20 minutes. Some gourmets seem to be of the opinion that periwinkles retain more of their natural flavor when roasted, but no matter which way you eat them, you will not be disappointed.

"Perry's" Winkles

1 pound periwinkles, in the shell	1 teaspoon salt
	¼ cup white wine
2 cups water	1 small onion, chopped

Place water in a large kettle, add periwinkles, salt, wine, and onion. Boil 20 minutes then serve hot with a melted butter dip. Each diner should pick the meat from a periwinkle with a pin or seafood fork, dip it in butter, and gulp it down whole. Serves 2.

GOOSE BARNACLES

There are several species of goose barnacle common to both the Atlantic and Pacific coasts of the U.S. The common west coast variety (Pellicipes polymerus) is somewhat larger in size than the east coast variety

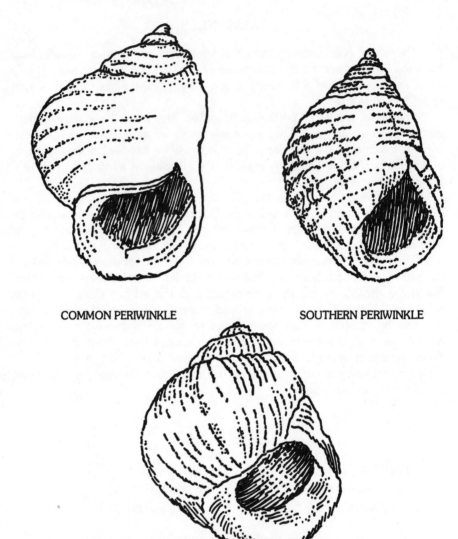

COMMON PERIWINKLE   SOUTHERN PERIWINKLE

BLUNT PERIWINKLE

PERIWINKLES

(Lepas fascicularis), but both are equally edible. A relative of the shrimp, both zoologically and in the matter of taste, the goose barnacle lives attached to rocks and other solid objects by their long stalk-like necks. The goose barnacle attains a size of from 2 to 6 inches in length on our shores, but varieties from nine inches to a foot long are often found in South American waters, where they are a well recognized food.

Finding a supply of goose barnacles is not difficult. They live in prodigious numbers on rocks, pilings, ship bottoms, and just about anywhere where they can get a firm grip on a solid object. To gather the goose barnacle, simply cut their stalks down close to where they are attached.

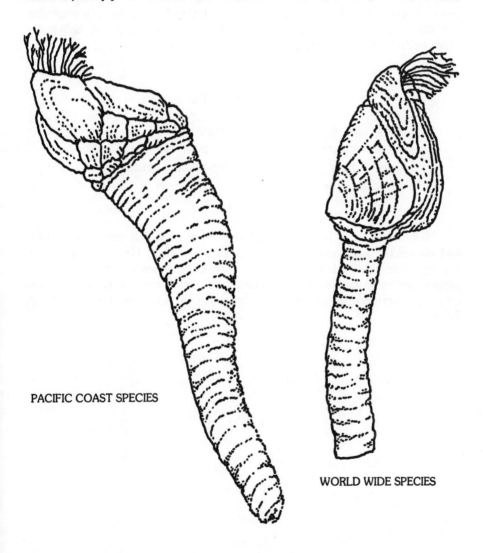

PACIFIC COAST SPECIES

WORLD WIDE SPECIES

GOOSE BARNACLES

Wash them thoroughly under cold running water and then steam them whole for 15 minutes in a covered pot containing just a bit of water in the bottom. Once cooked, they should be cleaned by removing the shells and disposing of the feathery like legs. Next peel away the tough outer skin from the stalks. What remains is the delicate pinkish-colored meat of the stalk which can be used as a substitute ingredient in many shellfish recipes. Chopped into small pieces and used instead of clams in a chowder, you will find this meat excellent. It is also excellent in dishes calling for either crab, lobster, or shrimp.

Barnacle Bill On Toast

1 cup barnacle meat,
  cooked and cleaned
2 tablespoons flour
2 tablespoons butter

1½ cups milk
½ teaspoon salt
½ cup cooked corn,
  whole kernel

Toast

Melt butter in a saucepan. Remove from heat and stir in flour until well blended. Place mixture back over very low heat. Gradually add milk, stirring each time mixture thickens until it becomes smooth. Add salt, pepper, barnacle meat and corn. Continue cooking until barnacle meat and corn are heated through (do not boil). Serve hot over buttered toast. Serves 2.

Chapter Eleven

General Information

AVOIDING TROUBLE

THERE IS little to worry about in regard to food poisoning when eating shellfish caught within the temperate waters of the continental United States, Canada, or Alaska. All you need do is follow the few simple precautions outlined here.

Shellfish are highly susceptible to pollution, and the best way to avoid this man-made menace, is by not eating shellfish taken from waters immediately adjacent to highly populated or highly industrialized areas. As a general rule, if the water is biologically safe enough for humans to swim in, then, shellfish taken from the area are safe to eat. Most areas in which it is unsafe to gather shellfish are usually posted by the federal or local agencies which enforce the shellfishing laws. Look carefully for these signs, but don't always count on seeing them. It is a good idea, when in a strange area, to make careful local inquiries about the safety of shellfishing in the area.

In addition to the above precautions, familiarize yourself with the following rules. Keep them in mind, and you will have little difficulty when engaged in the hunting of shellfish.

1. Only fresh shellfish, which are alive right up to the moment of cooking,

should be considered edible. All shellfish should look healthy and have a fresh, clean, untainted smell. The shells of clams, mussels, and other bivalves should always close up tightly when handled.

2. On the west coast of the United States, and in Alaska, make local inquiries as to when mussels are safe to gather. On the east coast, mussels are safe to eat at any time of the year.

3. When gathering mussels in any area, place them in a pail of water and discard those that float or gape open.

4. When hunting abalone, pry them loose from the rocks during periods of low tide only. Never use your bare hands to pry them off the rocks. Their powerful muscles can clamp down on an unwary hand and hold you there to be swallowed up by the incoming tide. Always use a heavy screwdriver or tire iron for prying loose abalone.

5. Don't handle jellyfish under any circumstances. Many of them are capable of inflicting severe stings.

6. When wading in unfamiliar waters, always wear something on your feet for protection from sharp shells, or some idiot's broken beer bottle (tennis shoes or sneakers are best).

7. Be careful when handling big conch shells. They can give you a jab that will make you howl.

THE WINES TO SERVE WITH SHELLFISH

The following is a list of wines you will find go equally well with almost any shellfish dish in this book.

Type of Wine	Serving Temperature	Taste
Chablis	Chilled	Dry
Champagne	Cold	Very dry
Haut Barzac	Well chilled	Sweet
Haut Sauterne	Well chilled	Sweet
Moselle	Chilled	Med dry
Rhine	Slightly chilled	Dry
Riesling	Slightly chilled	Dry
Sauterne	Chilled	Med dry
Sherry, dry	Slightly chilled	Extra dry
Sherry, golden	Room temperature	Med dry
Moselle, sparkling	Cold	Med dry
Sauterne, sparkling	Cold	Med dry
Burgundy, white	Chilled	Med dry
Chianti, white	Well chilled	Med dry
Port, white	Room temperature	Sweet

Red wines:
Rosé
Sparkling Burgundy   Slightly chilled   Very dry
Medoc

In cooking recipes, calling for wine as an ingredient, use a good grade of wine. The cheap "cooking sherry's" are not satisfactory for cooking shellfish.

TO POLISH SHELLS

If you want to put a high polish on a shell, that is virtually indestructible and everlasting, try this method. It will make your shells all the more attractive to use as dishes, ash trays, or just plain decorations.

Prepare a solution of ⅓ part Muriatic acid (available at drug stores) and ⅔ parts water. Place this solution into a large porcelain or pyrex saucepan, and bring to a boil. Grasp shell with tongs and dip into the boiling mixture for about 10 seconds; then immediately plunge into ice water. This method works best on shells that are fairly hard, which most are.

THE SHELLFISH VERSUS THE CALORIE

It takes the following portions of shellfish to equal 120 calories:

1 boiled lobster, ¾ to 1 pound in weight
1 dozen oysters, including their juice
½ dozen scallops, muscles only
14 to 18 medium-sized shrimp
1 cup crab meat, cooked
9 medium-sized clams

From viewing this list you can see that shellfish are desirable for those who count calories. But let's go a step further, and look at the caloric count in a more practical way, which, of course, would be to look at the calories in an average serving of each shellfish.

Shellfish	Average Serving	Calories (Approx.)
Lobster (boiled)	¾ to 1 pound	120
Scallops (fried)	1 dozen	300
Oysters (fried)	1 dozen	350
Crab meat (boiled)	¾ cup	90
Clams (steamed)	10 to 12	150
Shrimp (canned)	4 to 6	50

Of course, the addition of such items as, for example, 1 tablespoon of butter to the above servings would add an additional 100 calories to each serving. In addition, 1 ounce of cheese would add another 100 or so calories; an egg, 75 calories; ½ pint of milk, 175 calories; 2 tablespoons of light cream, 60 calories; and 1 cup of flour, about 40 calories. From this you can see that a complete shellfish dish, utilizing more than just the plain shellfish alone, is not necessarily a low calories meal.

SHELLFISH CONSERVATION AND THE LAW

In most areas there is a reasonable limit to the number of shellfish that may be legally taken, and you will find it safest to stay within that limit.

Laws vary in different localities, but those prevailing in New England are fairly representative of most areas, and are the laws which I describe here, unless I am referring to a species which is unavailable there. In such cases, I pass along the laws in force in that locality at present.

The various laws and conservation practices which should be strictly followed by all shellfishermen are as follows:

Oysters should only be gathered in the months of September through April. They should be a minimum of three inches in length.

Hard-shelled clams (quahogs) should be no less than two inches in their longest direction. The same size also applies to the soft-shelled clams (steamers) in order to meet with most legal requirements. The amount of hard or soft-shelled clams that may be dug each day in each area may differ widely, so be sure to check on the laws with the local authorities.

When digging clams, please be kind enough to fill in the holes you have left behind, so that the baby clams you have left behind in those holes will have a chance to survive. If you neglect this practice, they will quickly become food for their prey on the incoming tide, or scooped up by the seagulls as soon as you leave the area. Taking care of the babies will help you to insure a supply of clams the next time you return to the area.

Scallops must have a one year's growth ring showing, and generally may not be taken during the months of January through September.

In some areas, crabs must measure five inches across the widest part of the shell to be of legal size, while in other areas there are no restrictions as to size or numbers that may be taken. In all areas it is usually against the law to keep any female crab bearing eggs. Egg bearing females can be recognized by the spongy looking sacs hanging from the front of the crab.

Lobsters are mainly the concern of commercial fishermen, and there is no specific season in which it is not legal to catch or trap them. If you plan to engaged in trapping lobsters, make inquiries into the local laws as regards licenses and legal lobster sizes. These laws vary from state to state. Under no circumstances is it legal to keep a female lobster bearing eggs. These can be immediately recognized by the dark mass of small eggs covering the underside of the lobsters tail. Egg bearing lobsters should be treated most tenderly and immediately placed gently back into the sea.

I know of no state which presently regulates the gathering of mussels. However, it is important for you to make local inquiries before taking mussels along the Pacific coast. In this part of the country, mussels are generally quarantined during the months of May through October.

Most of the laws pertaining to the miscellaneous shellfish mentioned in this book, are included in the section describing that particular shellfish. For such shellfish as the whelks, winkles, conch, coquina, moon snails, etc., I know of no regulations that limit catching them. Do however, treat all shellfish with the respect that nature is due. Don't take more than you can use, and don't destroy, litter, or pollute the areas which you visit during your shellfish foraging.

Keep in mind that it is always the individual shellfish collector upon whom the great responsibility of conservation rests. As a group, we must always be conscientious enough not to disturb the seashore any more than is absolutely necessary. It is very easy to disturb the delicate balance of nature along a stretch of seashore. All one need do is walk down a beach turning over every rock in sight and slinging around clumps of seaweed, etc., to totally and irreversibly destroy the ecological balance of that beach. It can turn from a live beach to a dead one in a few short days, in fact almost overnight in most cases.

We must only take what we can use. Never, never, clean out a colony, and never get into the habit of being a "Bushel-Basket" collector just because supplies seem plentiful and easy to gather.

Almost all states protect edible and commercially valuable shellfish by requiring a license to gather them, and enforcing restrictions on numbers and size that may be taken. Find out what these laws are and follow them. If you have a secret shellfishing location, treat it with respect and your secret mine will remain as valuable as a gold mine, producing food for your table year in and year out.

GUIDE TO FREEZING SHELLFISH

If you desire to store shellfish for prolonged periods, freezing is the answer. It is most desirable to freeze shellfish while still as fresh as possible because they tend to deteriorate rather quickly and go downhill as regards flavor and quality. The following methods are generally considered the best ones to employ in freezing the "big five" favorite shellfish products that are commonly dealt with in the average kitchen.

Clams

Shuck fresh clams as soon as possible and save the liquid. Wash meat in salted water, drain well, then rinse in cold, fresh water. Pack into freezer containers and cover with their natural juice. If you have not saved enough natural juice, use a brine made with ⅓ cup of salt to 1 gallon of water.

The recommended storage time for frozen clams is from 4 to 5 months.

Crabs

Prepare fresh crabs for freezing immediately upon getting them home. Wash under cold running water, then cook in salted water (½ teaspoon to 1 quart water) for 20 minutes. Cool as quickly as possible. Shell the crabs and pick out all their meat. Pack in freezer containers and store in the coldest part of the freezer.

The recommended storage time for fresh frozen crab meat is 3 to 5 months. Note: Frozen crab meat is apt to be a bit tougher than fresh crab meat.

Lobsters

You can freeze whole, live lobsters, but I do not recommend the practice as the meat becomes much more difficult to remove from the shells when you finally do cook them. The best procedure is to plunge live lobsters into boiling salted water for 2 to 3 minutes, just long enough to cook the meat next to the shell. Cool quickly, and freeze them right in the shell. Prepared in this way, whole lobsters can be taken right from the freezer, plunged into boiling water for 20 minutes or so and served in the shell, just as with live, fresh lobsters.

Another method of freezing lobster meat, is to cook the lobsters for 20 minutes in salted water, just as if you were preparing them to be served immediately. After cooking, pick out the meat from the shells, package in freezer containers and freeze. For best results, don't store frozen lobster meat for much more than 2 months.

Oysters

Prepare oysters for the freezer just as you would clams. Use only fresh oysters. Those which have been kept on ice for several days are generally not of good enough quality to bother freezing. If you use fresh oysters they will retain their best qualities if used up within 2 to 3 months time.

Scallops

It is very important with scallops, just as with oysters, to use only the freshest for freezing. Shuck scallops, but don't bother to save their juice as it is not required for the freezing process. Pack scallop meat tightly in freezer containers, seal tightly, and store in the coldest part of your freezer. Scallops will retain their sweet quality and nutritional value if used within 3 to 4 months.

Shrimp

Whole fresh shrimp are prepared for the freezer by first removing the head from the body. This is usually done with a sharp knife and care should be taken with the sharp horn on the shrimp's head. Wash shrimp thoroughly in cold water after removing the heads, making certain that all possible grit has been removed.

Place the shrimp in a container and cover with cold water and a generous amount of ice cubes for about 30 minutes. This chilling process will hasten the freezing and contribute to a fresher tasting shrimp when finally cooked.

Drain the ice water from the chilled shrimp and place into tightly covered freezer containers. Freeze for 24 hours. Then remove the shrimp from the freezer and fill each container with ice water. Reseal the containers tightly and return immediately to the freezer.

Frozen shrimp treated in this way will be hard to tell from the fresh product when thawed and cooked. Recommended storage time for frozen shrimp is 3 to 4 months. The shrimp, however, will begin to toughen and lose some of their taste after the first week.

If properly wrapped, your frozen shellfish will not impart a fishy flavor or odor to other foods stored in your freezer.

Shellfish which are frozen immediately after leaving the ocean, are vastly superior to shellfish which have been on ice for a few days in the fish market. Unless you are dealing with strictly fresh caught shellfish, the freshly frozen product will be the next best thing.

Always keep shellfish frozen solidly until ready for use. After you have thawed out a container of frozen shellfish, don't refreeze it under any circumstances. The proper temperature for frozen shellfish storage is zero degrees or below.

Shellfish should always be thoroughly defrosted prior to cooking or they will become tough. The recommended method is to defrost them in the refrigerator until soft and pliable enough to handle. Never thaw shellfish at room temperature as spoilage may result when the thinner portions have thawed and thicker parts are still frozen solid.

Use tightly sealed packages or containers to store all shellfish in the freezer. Improperly sealed packages will contribute to a loss of moisture, and cause the shellfish to eventually dry out and shrink.

Fresh shellfish may be stored in the coldest section of a refrigerator for short periods of time. The temperature should be just at 32 degrees F.— anything higher than that will cause a surprising loss of quality in just a few short hours.

BEACHCOMBERS GUIDE TO THE CURIOUS

While roaming along the seashore in search of shellfish, you may occasionally come across some curious objects, cast up on the beach by the tides, that are unfamiliar to you. It seems appropriate to include a few of those items in this book, and give a brief explanation of each, to help satisfy your curiosity and perhaps encourage you to study the seashore and its most fascinating natural history further.

Sand Dollars

The sand dollars, which are commonly found along most beaches, are actually the skeletons of a type of sea urchin. This particular type of urchin lives on sandy bottoms, just off-shore surf pounded beaches. Their flat bodies have apparently been evolved for the purpose of presenting as streamlined a surface as possible to the actions of the waves, currents, and shifting sands. Once these animals die, they loose their outer structures and their skeletal remains eventually get washed up upon the beaches.

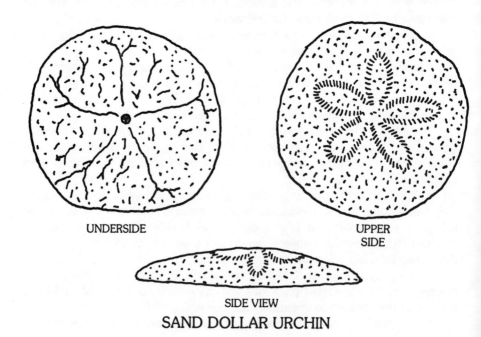

UNDERSIDE   UPPER
                             SIDE

SIDE VIEW

SAND DOLLAR URCHIN

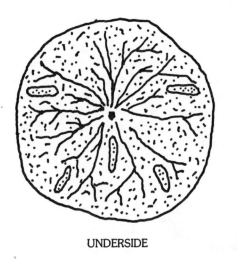 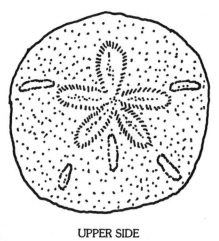

UNDERSIDE   UPPER SIDE

KEYHOLE URCHIN

Skate Eggs

The illustration below is likely a familiar object to those who do any walking along beaches in summer months. These pillow-like, leathery objects are the cases in which skates and rays lay their eggs. After the young skates have hatched, these cases float ashore and become part of the common beach litter of the summer season. These egg cases are variously known as "sea purses" or "devil's pocketbooks," and may be from 2 to 6 inches in length, either blackish or dark green in color. The spikes on either end of the case serve to hold it anchored to some solid object during the hatching period.

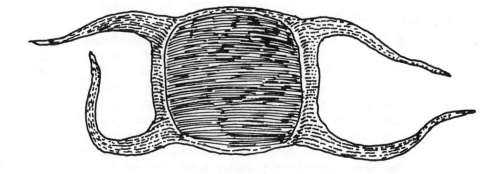

EGG CASE OF THE SKATE FISH

Sand Collars

These extremely delicate objects often found on sandy beaches are the eggs of the moon shell snail. This animal lays its eggs in a mass of jelly, which it molds around its shell to form a collar. Sand particles soon begin to adhere to the outside of the jelly-like mass, and when hardened, form the "sand collars" that are occasionally washed up on the beach. These objects are from 2 to 10 inches in diameter, but because they are so fragile they are seldom found in a whole condition.

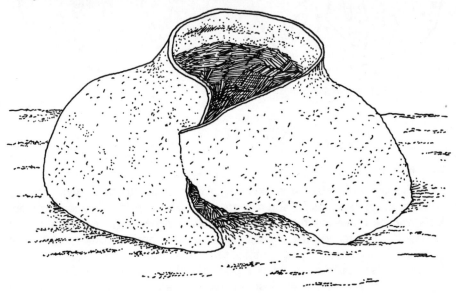

SAND COLLAR

Sea Urchin Shells (spiny variety)

These delicate little globular shells with a circular opening on their slightly flattened bottoms, are the skeletal remains of the common spiny sea urchins, which inhabit the rocky areas just below the low tide line. It is the little hole on the bottom in which the mouth of the live animal is located. This mouth consists of a complicated arrangement of teeth-like plates, which is called "Aristotle's lantern" by zoologists.

Beachcombers like to collect the sea urchin shells and fill them with plaster of paris to serve as paper weights. They also make grand miniature lamp shades when used with tiny electric bulbs. You will be fascinated by the many unexpected colors these miniature lamp shades reveal.

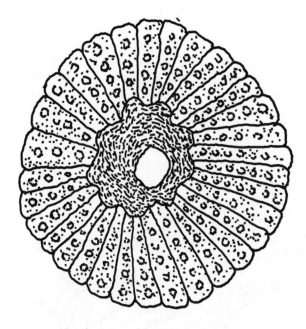

SPINY SEA URCHIN SHELL

Whelk Eggs

The illustration below is another common sight to most shoreline strollers. These long strings of disc-like objects are the egg cases of the whelk. Sometimes you can open up the little discs and find tiny whelk shells inside.

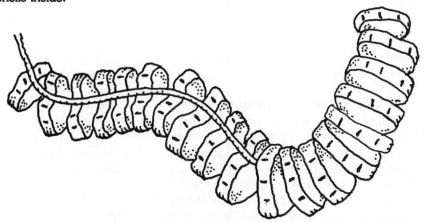

EGG CASES OF THE WHELK

Sea Mouse

Another odd looking creature you may find washed up on the beach is the sea mouse. This little scamp is usually from 3 to 6 inches long and has brightly colored green and gold hair like a mouse, with brownish spines. The sea mouse is actually a member of the worm family and lives on muddy or sandy bottoms in shallow water.

SEA MOUSE

Many thanks for staying with me to the end. The subject of this book, of course, has been shellfish, mainly those which can be easily gathered, employing only simple equipment at the edge of the sea. For this reason, I have not made mention of such delicacies as shrimp, which are not easily gathered along the seashore without specialized equipment such as power boats, nets, or specialized local knowledge.

I have used the term shellfish throughout the book to loosely describe all creatures with a shell or shell-like covering, whether they be mollusks, crustaceans, or other classification. I trust that I have not confused anyone by lumping all these things together and calling them shellfish.

VARIOUS TOOLS USED FOR OPENING SHELLFISH

QUAHOGS

SCALLOPS

OYSTERS

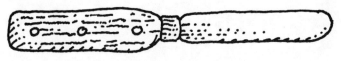

CLAMS

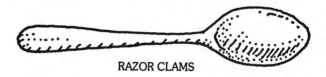

RAZOR CLAMS

Where should you go to gather shellfish? My suggestion would be, just about anywhere. The vast amount of coastline readily available to Americans is equal to about five times the distance around the world, and contrary to popular belief, much of it is still uncrowded, undeveloped and teeming with delicious things to eat. I hope this book will inspire you to seek out and explore some of this coastline. While you are there, seek out some of its delicacies, and listen to the fascinating story that nature has to tell those who will listen.

A Short Glossary of Shell Terms

Anterior end—In bivalve shells this is the opposite end to which the ligament is attached—the front of the animal in life.

Aperture—The opening of a shell—in snails the entrance to the body whorl.

Bivalve—Composed of two pieces (Shells)

Byssus—The threads manufactured by certain bivalves which are used for attachment to solid objects.

Gastropods—Univalve shells such as snails, conchs, whelks, etc.

Gibbous—Hump backed.

Globose—Globular, or nearly so.

Hinge—Point of connection between shell valves.

Mantle—The fleshy covering of the body, next to the shell; secretes the material from which the shell is formed.

Mouth—Aperture of a univalve shell—as regards the animal itself, the mouth is the portion where nourishment is taken.

Operculum—A hard shelly plate which closes off the aperture of many snails when the animal retreats inside its shell.

Siphon—Tubes of bivalve animals used for taking in clear water and discharging waste materials.

Umbo—The beginning of a bivalve shell.

Glossary of Cooking Terms

In the recipes presented in this book, a pinch or a dash denotes an amount less than ⅛ teaspoon; a pinch being perhaps a bit larger an amount than a dash.

All measurements, whether cup, teaspoon, tablespoon, pint, quart, etc., are level measurements, unless otherwise indicated.

A pinch or a dash = less than ⅛ teaspoon
1 dessert spoon = 2 teaspoons
1 teaspoon = ⅓ tablespoon
1 tablespoon = 3 teaspoons = ½ liquid ounce
1 liquid ounce = 2 tablespoons = ⅛ cup
¼ cup = 4 tablespoons
⅓ cup = 5 tablespoons plus 1 teaspoon
1 cup = ½ liquid pint = 8 liquid ounces = 16 tablespoons
1 pint = 2 cups = ½ quart = 16 ounces = 32 tablespoons
1 quart = 2 pints = 4 cups = 32 fluid ounces